Complete Audio-Typing: Student's Book
A Programmed Course

Marion Prescott, B.A.(Hons), M.Sc.(Econ), M.B.I.M.,
Head of Department of Office Studies
South East London College

PITMAN PUBLISHING
128 Long Acre, London WC2E 9AN

A Division of Longman Group UK Limited

© Longman Group Limited 1974, 1986

First published in Great Britain 1974
Second Edition 1986
Reprinted 1988, 1991

British Library Cataloguing in Publication Data
Prescott, Marion
    Complete audio typing. – 2nd ed.
    Student's book
    1. Typewriting – Problems, exercises, etc.
    I. Title
    652.3' 07   Z49.2

ISBN 0 273 02543 0

Acknowledgements

I should like to thank my colleagues in the Inner
London service for their help, encouragement and co-

operation in validating the material.
I should also like to thank the Royal Society of Arts
for their kind permission to reproduce examination
papers in Audio Typewriting.

Produced by Longman Singapore Publishers (Pte) Ltd.
Printed in Singapore

Contents

TB = Teacher's book only

Unit 1 – Short sentences   Notes   1
Preliminary listening practice   1
Task 1:1   Model on page   29
Task 1:2   29
Production Task A   TB
Task 1:3   29
Task 1:4   29

Unit 2 – Longer sentences   Notes   2
Task 2:1   30
Task 2:2   30
Production Task B   TB
Task 2:3   30
Task 2:4   30

Unit 3 – Short paragraphs and capital letters   Notes   3
Task 3:1   31
Task 3:2   31
Reference Section 1 is on   75
Task 3:3   31
Production Task C   TB
Task 3:4   31

Unit 4 – Short paragraphs using plurals   Notes   4
Task 4:1   32
Reference Section 2 is on   76
Task 4:2   32
Production Task D   TB
Task 4:3   32

Unit 5 – Use of the comma   Notes   5
Task 5:1   33
Reference Section 3 is on   76
Task 5:2   33
Production Task E   TB
Task 5:3   33

Unit 6 – Letter display   Notes   6
Task 6:1   34
Reference Section 4 is on   78
Task 6:2   34
Production Task F   TB
Task 6:3   35

Unit 7 – Letters: dictating conventions   Notes   7
Task 7:1   36
Reference Section 5 is on   80
Task 7:2   37
Task 7:3   38
Production Task G   TB

Unit 8 – Memo display; Indexing   Notes   8
Task 8:1   39
Reference Section 6 is on   81
Task 8:2   39
Production Task H   TB
Task 8:3   40
Reference Section 7 is on   82
Task 8:4   41
Task 8:5   42

Unit 9 – Use of apostrophe; Homophones   Notes   9
Task 9:1   43
Reference Section 8 is on   83
Task 9:2   44
Production Task I   TB
Task 9:3   45
Reference Section 9 is on   84
Task 9:4   46
Production Task J   TB

Unit 10 – Drafts; Circulars; Reports   Notes   10
Task 10:1   47
Task 10:2   48
Production Task K   TB
Task 10:3   49
Task 10:4   50

Unit 11 – RSA I Examination paper   Notes   10
Practice   51
Reference Section 10 is on   85

Unit 12 – RSA I Examination paper   Notes   10
Production (Teacher's Book)   TB

Unit 13 – Dictated display; Corrections to dictated matter   Notes   17
Task 13:1   56
Task 13:2   57
Task 13:3   58
Production Task L   TB
Task 13:4   59

Unit 14 – Audio with tabular work; Composing letters from notes   Notes   18
Task 14:1   60
Reference Section 11 is on   86
Task 14:2   62
Production Task M   TB
Task 14:3   64
Reference Section 12 is on   87
Task 14:4   65
Production Task N   TB

Unit 15 – RSA II Examination paper   Notes   20
Practice   66

Unit 16 – RSA II Examination paper   Notes   20
Production (Teacher's Book)   TB

Reference Sections
1   Capital letters; Open punctuation   75
2   Plurals   76
3   Use of the comma   76
4   Letter display   78
5   Dictating conventions   80
6   Memo display   81
7   Indexing   82
8   The apostrophe   83
9   Similar-sounding words (homophones)   84
10 Examinations   85
11 Audio with tabular work   86
12 Writing letters from dictated notes   87

Preface

Complete Audio-Typing is a programmed course of instruction consisting of a Teacher's Book and a Student's Book.

The Student's Book is divided into three parts.

Part I. Notes to each Task. You should study these notes carefully before commencing each task. Further instructions may be given on the cassette.

Part II. Reference Sections. The 12 Reference Sections cover areas of work important to audio-typists. These can be taken by the class together or as private study.

Part III. Model Tasks. These are for use by you on completion of each task. It is important that you do not look at the Model Task before attempting each task, or you will not learn the work sufficiently well to cope with the Production Tasks. Every third or fourth task is a Production Task, and the Model Tasks to these are given only in the Teacher's Book.

Note on the use of commas. Commas are used extensively in the punctuation of the dictation material in the Teacher's Book as an aid to dictation. However, only the more important commas are shown in the Model Tasks in your book.

Note on Teacher's Book. A full discussion on the methods of teaching audio-typing and the use of this course is given in the introduction to the Teacher's Book. The Teacher's Book also gives the dictation material word for word using the RSA dictating conventions where appropriate, and the Models to the Production Tasks.

Notes to tasks

Always type the task number and your name at the top of each sheet of paper you use.

UNIT 1 — Short sentences

Preliminary listening practice

This is a listening task — you will not need to type anything. All the instructions are on the cassette. Start at the beginning of the cassette and listen carefully.

Spelling preview

enclosure	designs
manufacture	relevant
literature	attention
branches	locally
favourable	despatch*
advertisement	

* despatch/dispatch — either is correct, but you must be consistent. Keep to one spelling.

Task 1:1

You will now type five short sentences on plain A5 paper (or A4 folded in half). Use the long side of the paper at the top. Start at least six clear single-line spaces from the top of the paper and set your left-hand margin at 15. Set your machine for double-line spacing. Type one sentence at a time and do not begin to type a sentence until you have heard the whole of it. Start to type when you hear the words "full stop". Start each sentence on a new line but do not number them.

Task 1:2

Five short sentences — same instructions as for Task 1:1. **Remember: Eyes on your work — not on your fingers.**

Production Task A

Five short sentences — same instructions as for Task 1:1. The answers are not given in this book since your teacher will mark this task. You should audio-type it once only. **Do not copy or audio-type a second attempt.** Time yourself to see how many minutes you take and note this on the paper before handing it in to your teacher.

Task 1:3

Five short sentences — same instructions as for Task 1:1.

Task 1:4

Five short sentences — same instructions as for Task 1:1.

UNIT 2 — Long sentences

Spelling preview

receive*   competitor(s)
luxury   superior
trial   brochure(s)
variety   disappointed
inventory   location

*i before e except after c (Well, usually!)

Task 2:1

You will now type five long sentences on plain A5 paper. Use single-line spacing for each sentence, but turn up twice between sentences. Instead of listening to the whole sentence before beginning to type, you should start typing after you have heard the first long phrase (at which point the dictator will pause). But **before** you finish typing the first phrase, you should start your machine again and listen to the rest of the sentence, whilst continuing to type. If you do this successfully, you will be typing continuously. For example: The first sentence is:

> We have received your request concerning colour televisions and are enclosing full details.

You listen as far as the word "televisions" and then begin to type. But when you reach the word "request", you start your machine again and listen to the rest of the sentence — while continuing to type "for colour televisions" — and then type through to the end of the sentence without stopping. Thus, while typing the middle of the sentence, you are listening to the end of it. This skill will take practice.

Task 2:2

Five long sentences — same instructions as for Task 2:1.

Production Task B

Five long sentences — same instructions as for Task 2:1. Your teacher will mark this task. You should audio-type it once only. Time yourself and note this on the paper before handing it in.

Task 2:3

Five long sentences — same instructions as for Task 2:1.

Task 2:4

Five long sentences — same instructions as for Task 2:1.

UNIT 3 – Short paragraphs and capital letters

Spelling preview

appoint(ed)	potential
director(s)	loyalty
permanent	enthusiasm
consultant	literature

Task 3:1

You will now type three short paragraphs on A5 paper. Use single line spacing and blocked paragraphs. Turn up twice between paragraphs. These paragraphs are to be typed continuously: before you finish typing each long phrase (or short sentence) you should start your machine again and listen to the next section so that you type all the time until the paragraph is completed. The instruction for a new paragraph will be dictated.

Task 3:2

Three short paragraphs – same instructions as for Task 3:1. Some of the words dictated need capital letters, so before starting this task, look carefully at Reference Section 1 – Capital letters; Open punctuation. Names dictated are: John Brown, Harrow, Oxford Street, Birmingham.

Task 3:3

Three short paragraphs – same instructions as for Task 3:1. These paragraphs contain some instructions to use "initial capital(s)". Name dictated: Mr K Smith.

Production Task C

Three short paragraphs – same instructions as for Task 3:1. Your teacher will mark this task. You should audio-type it once only. Time yourself and note this on the paper before handing it in. Name dictated: British Products Limited. Passage refers to: Report and Accounts. These are important business documents produced each year by most organizations.

Task 3:4

Three short paragraphs – same instructions as for Task 3:1. Names dictated are: Avis, Hertz.

UNIT 4 — Short paragraphs using plurals

Spelling preview

processor	quartz
exclusive	electronic
believe	consignment
bankruptcy	personnel
media	computers

Task 4:1

Three short paragraphs — some of the words dictated are plural words. Use A5 paper, landscape (long side of the paper at the top). Before starting this task you should study Reference Section 2 — Plurals — in the book. Continue to keep to the blocked style, with single line spacing, double between paragraphs.

Task 4:2

Three short paragraphs — same instructions as for Task 4:1. These paragraphs contain some instructions to use "initial capital(s)". Names dictated are: Wang, IBM.

Production Task D

Three short paragraphs — same instructions as for Task 4:1. Your teacher will mark this task. You should audio-type it once only. Time yourself and note this on the paper before handing it in.

Task 4:3

Three short paragraphs — same instructions as for Task 4:1.

UNIT 5 – Use of the comma

Spelling preview

woollen	synthetics
terylene	accountancy
financial	succeed
computer	operator
technology	software
novelty	consumer
predecessors	cashpoint
previously	visual

Task 5:1

Three short paragraphs – continue to keep to the blocked style, with single-line spacing, double between paragraphs. You will now need to use the comma occasionally, so before you start you should study Reference Section 3 – Use of the comma. Names dictated are: Mr A North, Mr John Jackson.

Task 5:2

Three paragraphs – same display instructions as for Task 5:1. Names dictated are: Mrs Janice Roberts, Mr James Gordon.

Production Task E

Three paragraphs – same instructions as for Task 5:1. Your teacher will mark this task. You should audio-type it once only. Time yourself and note this on the paper before handing it in.

Task 5:3

Three paragraphs – same instructions as for Task 5:1.

UNIT 6 — Letter display

Spelling preview

electronic	overdraft
drastically	facility
mortgage	assurance
solicitor	offset

Note: Names will no longer be given to you in advance. They will, however, be spelled out if they are at all unusual by the person dictating.

Task 6:1

This is a short letter (103 words). The address is as follows:

(with punctuation)	(open punctuation)
Mrs. C. Thompson,	Mrs C Thompson
23 Dorset Gardens,	23 Dorset Gardens
Bournemouth	Bournemouth
BH2 1NH	BH2 1NH

Use A5 paper, with suitable margins. If you have pica type (the larger one) and are using the fully-blocked style, turn up twice only between the reference, date, address and salutation — or you will not fit the letter on A5. Before beginning to type, check letter display in Reference Section 4 — Letter display. The reference is MW/BB. Take one carbon copy. Don't forget today's date. If you do not have headed paper, remember to leave a suitable space at the top of the paper to allow for this. With A5, about ten single line spaces is sufficient.

Task 6:2

This is a short letter (89 words) to:

(with punctuation)	(open punctuation)
Mr. C. Hatchard, B.A.,	Mr C Hatchard BA
15 Royal Court,	15 Royal Court
Haywards Ave.,	Haywards Ave
Watford WD3 6QR	Watford WD3 6QR

Use A5 paper. The reference is MEM/2371

Production Task F

This is a letter of 109 words to:

(with punctuation)	(open punctuation)
Turner & Black Ltd.,	Turner & Black Ltd
34 — 38 Belding Road,	34 — 38 Belding Road
Huddersfield	Huddersfield
HD2 3MA	HD2 3MA

Use A5 paper. The reference is KAB/your initials. If you have pica type, make full use of the space available (narrow margins, start close to the letter heading). Do not forget the date, or the carbon copy. Your teacher will mark this task. Audio-type it once only, and time yourself.

Task 6:3

This is a letter of 92 words to:

(with punctuation)	(open punctuation)
Mr. and Mrs. D. Piper,	Mr and Mrs D Piper
62 Spring Street,	62 Spring Street
LONDON	LONDON
N1 4AN	N1 4AN

UNIT 7 — Letters: dictating conventions

Spelling preview

Parliament	crockery
theme	liable
European	breakages
subsequent	luncheon
appointment	vouchers
occasion	consecutively
believe	personnel
appreciate	

Task 7:1

Before attempting this task you should study Reference Section 5 — RSA Dictating Conventions. In this letter the following new instructions, as listed below, will be dictated and guidance for these can be found in the numbered paragraphs of Reference Section 5.

capital letters —	see Reference Section 5 para 13
colon —	see Reference Section 5 para 2
question mark —	see Reference Section 5 para 2
open single quotes	
. . . close quotes —	see Reference Section 5 para 4

This letter is longer so you should use A4 paper. Continue to take one carbon copy and use today's date. Reference DK/your initials. The letter is to Mrs E Small, MP, Constituency Headquarters, Bridge Road, London, SW18 4JB. Pay attention to the punctuation of the address when displaying it in the letter.

Task 7:2

In this letter the new instructions, listed below, will be dictated. See Reference Section 5 — Dictating conventions — numbered paragraphs for guidance.

dash —	see Reference Section 5 para 2

semi-colon —	see Reference Section 5 para 2
hyphen —	see Reference Section 5 para 2

Use A4 paper with normal margins. The letter is to The Manager, Universal Appliances Limited, Endsleigh House, London, W6 8HH. Reference RG/your initials.

Task 7:3

In this letter the new instructions, set out below, will be dictated. See the numbered paragraphs in Reference Section 5 — Dictating conventions.

stop — used with	
figures —	see Reference Section 5 para 13
oblique —	see Reference Section 5 para 5
underscore —	see Reference Section 5 para 10
P (for Peter) —	see Reference Section 5 para 8

Use A4 paper. The letter is to Northern Wholesalers Ltd, 180 Great Western Way, Manchester, M1 2DG. The letter is for the attention of Mr W Price. (If necessary, check from Reference Section 4 — Letter display — to see where to place an "attention" line.) Our reference is Sales/23/PLJ. Their reference is WP/MM.

Production Task G

In this letter the following new instructions will be dictated:

words —	see Reference Section 5 para 11
pound sign —	see Reference Section 5 para 12
open brackets . . .	
close brackets —	see Reference Section 5 para 4
name spelt out —	see Reference Section 5 para 8

The letter is to Miss P Jeffries, 46 Laburnum Road, Croydon, Surrey, CR4 2BB. Reference PERS/ID/your initials. Use A4 paper. Do not forget the carbon copy and today's date. Time yourself. Your teacher will mark this task.

UNIT 8 — Memo display; Indexing

Spelling preview

associate	allocate
grateful	seniority
stationery (paper, etc.)	priority
arrears	shop-floor

Task 8:1

Before attempting this task, you should study Reference Section 6 — Memo display (read the memos addressed to you). When you are ready to type, you will need A5 paper, with the long side at the top. If you use a memo form, make sure that your typing is slightly above any dotted lines you have to complete. Do not forget the carbon copy and today's date. The reference is MS/EF.

Task 8:2

Memo. Use a form, if possible: A5 paper, Reference LW/PP.

Production Task H

Memo. Reference MN/POJ. Do not forget the carbon copy or today's date. A5 paper. This will be marked by your teacher: time yourself.

Task 8:3

Before attempting this task, you should study Reference Section 7 — Indexing. You must decide on paper size and margins. The letter is to Mr R Richardson, 25 Regent Street, Wolverhampton, WV2 4DB. Reference ACCTS/LQ/your initials.

Task 8:4

Memo. Reference PERS/LE/KK.

Task 8:5

Letter to Mr L Kimpton, 48 North Street, Coventry, CV1 5RS. Our ref. JH/your initials.

UNIT 9 — Use of apostrophe; Homophones

Spelling preview

unanimously	labourers
punctually	disappear
absence	

Task 9:1

Before attempting this task, you should carefully study Reference Section 8 — The apostrophe. This is a passage which should be typed in double-line spacing with indented paragraphs. Because of the double-line spacing, you will need A4 paper. It has a centred heading in closed capitals, underscored, "John Constable and Company Limited". If necessary, see Reference Section 5 — Dictating conventions — para 9 about headings.

The answers to the task at the end of Reference Section 8 are: company's; director's; secretaries'; women's; month's.

Task 9:2

This is a memo testing use of the apostrophe. It contains five numbered items. You may use any suitable method of display of these items. If using the fully-blocked style, the recommended method is to type the numbers at the margin: block and inset the numbered paragraphs. Use A4 size paper.

Production Task I

This is a letter to Miss G Bolch, 15 Long Street, London, SW8 4ES. Their reference GB/OT. Our reference SALES/RJT. Type this task once only. Time yourself. Your teacher will mark this task.

Task 9:3

Before you attempt this task you should study Reference Section 9 which deals with homophones (similar-sounding words). This task is a letter to Mrs P Josephs of 16 Watford Way, Kingston-upon-Thames, Surrey, KT4 3DS. Ref. JJ/QWM.

The answers to the task in Reference Section 9 are: principal; ensure; licence; passed; licence; adverse; weather; affect; cereals; Council; their; differ; check; whether; site. If you got any of these wrong, you should look up the meanings of the words in your dictionary before proceeding.

Task 9:4

This is a memo containing a number of homophones. The reference is KT/MP.

Production Task J

This is a passage with a centred heading testing a number of homophones. Use double-line spacing. Do not forget the carbon copy. Type this task once only. Time yourself. Your teacher will mark this task.

UNIT 10 — Drafts; Circulars; Reports

Spelling preview

bankrupt
informants
cautious
maintenance
campaign

queue
congestion
voluntarily
multi-ethnic
delicacy

Task 10:1

This is a draft letter. Unless otherwise instructed, you type drafts in double-line spacing, to facilitate correction and amendment. If you have to go on to a continuation sheet, number it as usual. There is no need for an address, reference or date at the draft stage, unless there are specific instructions for these. No carbon is required. The word "DRAFT" should be typed at the top of the paper.

Task 10:2

Circular letter. In an office this would be typed on an offset litho plate, stencil or other "master", or keyed into a word processor to be merged with a mailing list. Display as if typing the master copy. Display of circular letters varies: some are dated, some use the month and year only and others bear the words "Date as Postmark". For a small circulation, space is often left for insertion of the name and address of the addressee and for a signature. With a large circulation, however, the addresses are not usually inserted (imagine doing this for, say 5,000 copies!) and the signature itself is duplicated in some way. In an examination you are usually told which form of circular letter you are to type. For Task 10:2 **do not** leave space for insertion of name and address. Use A5 paper. Date as Postmark. No carbon copy required.

Production Task K

Draft for circular letter — leave space for insertion of addressee details. Use A4 paper — no carbon copy required. Date with month and year only. Type this task once only. Time yourself. Your teacher will mark this task.

Task 10:3

A Staff Notice to be typed in double-line spacing on plain A4 paper.

Task 10:4

A newspaper report to be typed in double-line spacing on A4.

UNITS 11 and 12 — RSA I Examination papers

Before attempting these examination papers please read Reference Section 10 — Examinations.

Unit 11 — March 1983

On page 12 you will find the Notes for Candidates for this examination. The tasks are displayed for you to check at the end of each piece of work in the Model Tasks section of this book.

Unit 12 — May 1984

On page 15 the Notes for Candidates are printed as for the examination. Your teacher will mark these tasks. Time each task and at the end calculate how long you have taken overall. Hand the work to your teacher for marking.

Unit 11

THE ROYAL SOCIETY OF ARTS
EXAMINATIONS BOARD
SINGLE-SUBJECT EXAMINATIONS

AUDIO-TYPEWRITING, STAGE I
WEDNESDAY, 2nd MARCH 1983
Instructions to Candidates

(ONE HOUR AND FORTY MINUTES ALLOWED)

You have TEN minutes to read through this question paper before the start of the examination, during which time you may make notes on the examination paper.

2

INSTRUCTIONS TO CANDIDATES

PART I

On plain white paper type a corrected copy of the manuscript printed opposite.

(20 marks)

PART II

Except where a different instruction is given, all letters should be typed on the headed paper provided, ready for signature as for despatch today. Where no special directions are given regarding display, any method, consistently used within each exercise, will be accepted. Carbon copies should be taken only where indicated. Dictionaries may be used.

Passage 1   A circular letter. Leave space at the top of the letter for date, and name and
(26 marks)   address of addressee to be inserted. Indicate enclosures.

Passage 2   A notice to be typed on plain white paper. Heading: SITE SAFETY '83 –
(16 marks)   CONSTRUCTION SAFETY EXHIBITION. At the foot of the notice type:
               S. Christopher, Safety Officer and today's date.

Passage 3   A letter to Henderson & James Ltd, 23 St Anne's Square, Hitchin, Herts
(21 marks)   SG5 1QB. Our ref: AS/883. Heading: CLARKE LIMITED – ADVERTISING
               SUPPLEMENT. Take a carbon copy on yellow paper and indicate enclosures.

Passage 4   A memorandum to Managing Director from Office Manager. Heading:
(17 marks)   PORTABLE CABIN FOR TEMPORARY OFFICE ACCOMMODATION.
               Indicate enclosures.

N.B. *At the end of the examination you must insert all typewritten papers inside the cover of your answer book in the order of the examination paper and remain seated until this, together with the examination tape or disc, has been collected by the Invigilator.*

3

PART I

EARLY NOVELS OF GREAT BRITISH WRITERS - CONTINUED

close up   All in hard back at £1 each (post and packing extra) Please use the order form on page 15.

trs   VIVIAN GREY   Benjamin DISRAELI, (1804 - 1881)

His plan to create a new political party fails and after a duel he leaves for adventures in Europe.

lc   MARY BARTON   GASKELL, Elizabeth CLEGHORN (1810 - 1865)

stet   Mary's admirer is shot dead. Her lover is accused and tried; she desperately strives to save him.

OLIVER TWIST   DICKENS, Charles (1812 - 1870)

The story of a boy, born in a workhouse, who runs away to London and falls in with a gang of thieves.

CAPS   VANITY FAIR   Thackeray, William Makepeace (1811 - 1863)

run on   The contrasting life-stories of two girls: Becky Sharp is hard and clever but poor, whereas Amelia Sedley is gentle, dull & rich.

Page 5

Unit 12

THE ROYAL SOCIETY OF ARTS
EXAMINATIONS BOARD
SINGLE-SUBJECT EXAMINATIONS

AUDIO-TYPEWRITING, STAGE I
TUESDAY, 8th MAY 1984

(ONE HOUR AND FORTY MINUTES ALLOWED)

INSTRUCTIONS TO CANDIDATES

You have TEN minutes to read through this question paper before the start of the examination, during which time you may make notes on the examination paper.

A-TI(Cand)(Whitsun 1984)

(OVER)

2

INSTRUCTIONS TO CANDIDATES

PART I

On plain white A4 paper type a corrected copy of the manuscript printed opposite.

(20 marks)

PART II

Except where a different instruction is given, all letters should be typed on the headed paper provided, ready for signature as for despatch today. Where no special directions are given regarding display, any method, consistently used within each exercise, will be accepted.

Carbon copies should be taken only where indicated. Dictionaries and calculators may be used.

Passage 1
(26 marks)   A letter to Miss S Lawson, 49 Princes Avenue, Hull HU6 7DR. Our ref: SR/KG. Please type the name of the Personnel Officer (S Robinson) and his designation at the end of the letter and indicate the enclosure.

Passage 2
(16 marks)   A memorandum from Personnel Manager to Karen Green.

Passage 3
(18 marks)   An article to be typed in double (or 1½) line-spacing on plain white A4 paper. Heading: LANDSCAPING AND DISPLAY OF PLANTS IN OFFICES

Passage 4
(20 marks)   A letter to Mr D Edwards, Computer Management plc, 244 Heads Road, Grimsby, South Humberside DO30 16DP. It contains three numbered items. Please take a carbon copy on the yellow paper provided.

N.B. *At the end of the examination you must insert all typewritten papers inside the cover of your answer book in the order of the examination paper and remain seated until this, together with the examination tape or disc, has been collected by the Invigilator.*

3

PART I

PRAXITELES LANDSCAPE GARDENERS

Supreme Sale of Plants & Bulbs

Come Early! — SPACED CAPS

SAT 19 MAY 1984, 10 am – 2 pm

in the Main Hall, Central Ave, Scarborough

Typist: Please type the following in double-line spacing. Type in numbered order, but DO NOT type in numbers

(8) GLADIOLI CORMS (packs of 100) (28" high) — £1·00

(4) HONEYSUCKLE (scented varieties) — £1·50 each plant

(2) CLEMATIS PLANTS ([NELLY] nelly moser, Ville de Lyon, Jackmanii) — £1·25 each plant

(6) DOUBLE BEGONIAS (mixed) — 5 for £1

(1) HARDY AZALEAS (Various) — £1·25 each plant

(3) HARDY GARDEN CAMELLIAS (varied stock) — £1 each plant

(5) MAGNOLIA TREES — £6 each tree

(7) DECORATIVE & BORDER DAHLIAS (mixed colours) — 6 for £1·20

(9) MIXED SHRUBS (many varieties in stock) — from £1 each shrub

CAPS [Also a large collection of Annuals for summer flowering this season

LARGE CAR PARKS NEARBY

UNIT 13 — Dictated display; Corrections to dictated matter

Spelling — A preview will not be given from now on. Continue to use a dictionary for unfamiliar words.

Task 13:1

Circular letter which does not require space for insertion of addressee details. Date with month and year only. This letter contains short dictated information about cassettes of classical music, which should be displayed effectively. When information to be displayed is dictated in a letter or memo, it is advisable to listen through to the end of the items to be displayed, so that you can work out how best to display it. If the material is complicated, or involves columns of figures, it is probably easier to handwrite it quickly on a piece of rough paper, and then to work out the display.

Task 13:2

Letter to Mr L Machin, 18 Vera Way, Harlow, Essex, CM19 5BN. This letter contains short dictated information about hotels, which should be displayed effectively. A mistake was made in the dictation: a deposit on the booking should be **£10 per person, not £5** as dictated. The reference is JM/your initials.

In an office, correction may be indicated on the cassette itself or index strip (see Reference Section 7 — Indexing). In an examination, an instruction to make a correction may be printed with the notes to the task, as in this book. When you know a correction has to be made, listen ahead carefully to avoid typing the wrong version inadvertently.

Task 13:3

Memo, incorporating a dictated menu. Please note that **Tomato Soup, not Oxtail**, is on the menu. No carbon copy required, as this is for the Staff Noticeboard.

Production Task L

Memo. Take three carbon copies and when you have finished tick the names of the copies for circulation (the extra copy is for the file). Please note that the **meeting will be at 14.30 hrs, and not 14.00 hrs**, as dictated. This task should be typed once only and timed. Your teacher will mark this task.

Task 13:4

Letter to Mr V Graham, 6 Willow Court, 5—8 Gloucester Road, Exeter, Devon, EX5 4NU. Reference JKR/HJ/your initials. Use tomorrow's date. Please note that the **decorating work can start in three months' time, not two**, as dictated.

UNIT 14 – Audio with tabular work; Composing letters from notes

Task 14:1

Article about up-and-over garage doors. The table headed "EXCEL garage doors" accompanies this passage (Table for Task 14:1). Use double-line spacing for the article. Please see Reference Section 11 – Audio with tabular work – before commencing.

Task 14:2

This is a letter to Mrs A D Street, Westcliff College of Commerce, Straight Road, Westcliff-on-Sea, Essex, SSO 9LD. At the appropriate point, incorporate the list of books and book prices (Table for Task 14:2).

Production Task M

This is a memo. At the appropriate point in the dictation, incorporate the table headed "Sales Figures" given below. Type this task once only. Time yourself. Your teacher will mark this task.

Task 14:3

Notes will be dictated to you, from which you are to compose a reply to the letter which is Task 7:1 in your book. The letter is therefore to Mr D Kennedy. Before attempting this task, you should carefully study Reference Section 12 – Writing letters from dictated notes.

Task 14:4

Notes will be dictated in reply to the letter which is Task 7:3 in this book.

Production Task N

Notes will be dictated in reply to the letter which is Task 7:2 in this book. Do not spend more than 30 minutes on this task. Your teacher will mark your finished version.

Table 14.1   Excel garage doors

EXCEL GARAGE DOORS

| Type | Opening Size Height | | Weight | | Max thickness |
	Min	Max	Min	Max	
Modern	1740mm (5'9½")	2134mm (7'0")	27kg (60lb)	36kg (80lb)	51mm (2")
Traditional	1784mm (5'10¼")	2134mm (7'0")	27kg (60lb)	59kg (130lb)	51mm (2")
Country	1784mm (5'10¼")	2286mm (7'6")	59kg (130lb)	91kg (200lb)	57mm (2¼")

Note   For extreme ease of operation, and particularly by a short person, we recommend that the door height does not exceed 1981mm (6'6")

Table for Task 14:2

Order No	Quantity	Title & Author	Unit Price £	Total Price £
1641	50	Economic Theory by PW Bellamy	2.00	100.00
1653	30	Accounts & Auditing Practice by MS Chesterton	2.10	63.00
1666	18	Computer Programming Made Easy by Mary Green	4.80	86.40
"	10	Management Techniques by Paul Grey	1.50	15.00
"	15	Industrial Sociology by M M McKay	4.00	60.00
				324.40
Less 1631	50	Business Economics by P W Bellamy	1.60	80.00
				244.40

Table for Production Task M

Typist — Omit heading

SALES FIGURES

Area	Representative	Sales £	Increase/Decrease
London	Mr A Jepson	5,735	+421
Midlands	Mr R Couch	3,891	−403
N. Ireland	Mr F Shackleton	1,871	−118
North	Miss S Longbotham	2,872	−46
Scotland	Mr A McVeigh	1,976	+39
South East	Mrs D Collinson	5,942	+634
South West	Mr P Quiller	3,641	+48
Wales	Mr S Robertson	1,872	−34

UNITS 15 and 16 — RSA II Examination Papers

Before attempting these examination papers, please re-read Reference Section 10 — Examinations.

Unit 15 — June 1983

On page 21 you will find the Notes for Candidates for this examination. The tasks are displayed for you to check at the end of each piece of work in the Model Tasks section of this book.

Unit 16 — May 1984

On page 25 the Notes for Candidates are printed as for the examination. Your teacher will mark these tasks. Time each task, and at the end calculate how long you have taken overall. Hand the work to your teacher for marking.

Unit 15

THE ROYAL SOCIETY OF ARTS
EXAMINATIONS BOARD
SINGLE-SUBJECT EXAMINATIONS

AUDIO-TYPEWRITING, STAGE II
TUESDAY, 21st JUNE 1983
Instructions to Candidates

(TWO AND A HALF HOURS ALLOWED)

You have **TEN** minutes to read through this question paper before the start of the examination, during which time you may make notes on the examination paper.

IMPORTANT: *As soon as you receive this paper, read carefully the letter printed on page 4. Notes for a reply to this will be dictated to you as passage 8.*
   Except where a different instruction is given, all letters should be typed on the headed paper provided, ready for signature as for despatch today. Where no special directions are given regarding display, any method, consistently used within each exercise, will be accepted.
   Carbon copies should be taken only where indicated. Dictionaries may be used

Candidates must satisfy the examiner in each section of the examination.

2

Passage 1
(5 marks)

An article of 150 words about public relations. To be typed in double (or 1½) line-spacing on plain white paper. No heading is required.

Passage 2
(59 marks)

A letter to London Books PLC, Subscriptions Department, 8 The Leathermarket, London SE1 2EB. To be signed by Pamela Thrush, Secretary to Publications Manager. The publications list on page 3 of this paper is to accompany this letter.

Passage 3
(18 marks)

A letter to Miss Janet Cooper, American Technical Publications Corp, PO Box 2550, 88 Bedford Square, London WC1B 3FH. Our ref: LS/PT. Your ref: JC/22

Passage 4
(18 marks)

A letter to Mr V Godjal, Laine (PVT) Ltd, Padi, Madras, India 600 001. Please type the words AIR MAIL above the inside address.

Passage 5
(16 marks)

A letter to James Findlay, Findlay & Baker Ltd, 707 Retford Road, Sheffield, S1 3WH. Please take one carbon copy on the yellow paper provided.

Passage 6
(20 marks)

A memorandum from Secretary to Dr P R Henderson. Ref: JJT/PT. Heading: TABLING OF SUBCOMMITTEE REPORTS

Passage 7
(14 marks)

A letter to Mrs H Small, 120 Chestnut Avenue, Hereford HR2 6AZ. From the Customer Relations Department of Praxiteles Mail Order PLC.

Passage 8
(50 marks)

From the dictated notes, compose and type on headed paper a reply to the letter given on page 4.

NB. *At the end of the examination you must insert all typewritten papers inside the cover of your answer book in the order of the examination paper and remain seated until this, together with the examination tape or disc, has been collected by the Invigilator.*

3

Publications list to accompany Passage 2

BTRA - Publications   Price to
Members*

② Booklets

ⓧ lc Behaviour of Materials Under Stress   ~~75p~~ £1.00

ⓧ Quality Means Business   £~~1.00~~ 50

ⓧ Engineering Data on Materials (SI Units) £~~1.00~~ 50
              × (Imperial Units) £1.00

① BTRA Conference Books

ⓧ → uc The working Environment in Materials
Manufacturing Industries, 282 pp   £25.75

ⓧ Materials Technology for the '80s, 370 pp. £30.00

(A4 bound papers)

④ Periodicals

ⓧ Abstracts of International Materials Literature
(published bi-monthly)
Annual subscription payable in advance
(6 issues plus index)   £45.00

③ Broadsheets

ⓧ Technical information sheets - 200 titles
available - please send for full list

ⓧ Sets of 25 Broadsheets in ready-bound
           covers   £5.00

ⓧ Individual Broadsheets   50p each

ⓧ   ---   * Non-members
                               add 75%

ⓧ Please note zero rate VAT on all publications

ⓧ All prices include packing and postage

ⓧ Trade discount of 15% to booksellers

TYPIST — type in number order but do not type the
number. Double spacing where indicated ⓧ and
treble spacing between numbered sections.

4

Letter for reply — Passage 8

18 Elm Way
Bishampton
Pershore
Worcs WR10 2LX

10 June 1983

The Subscriptions Manager
Praxiteles Private Health Care Insurance
Praxiteles House
Adam Street
LONDON WC2N 6AJ

Dear Sir

Registration No 050846 — Scheme A

I write with reference to your recent notification of my renewal subscription, which I am surprised to find has increased from £139 to £192.

This very large increase of 38% is not reflected in the increases in benefits, nor is it in line with the rate of inflation. I should, therefore, be obliged if you would kindly check that the quoted subscription rate is correct, and if so please inform me as to the reasons for the very large increase.

I should also be pleased to receive a list of the subscription rates and benefits for all your schemes.

Yours faithfully

J J Green (Mrs)

Unit 16 (Model Answers to Tasks in this Unit are printed in the Teacher's book only)

THE ROYAL SOCIETY OF ARTS EXAMINATIONS BOARD
SINGLE-SUBJECT EXAMINATIONS

AUDIO-TYPEWRITING, STAGE II
TUESDAY, 15th MAY 1984
TWO AND A HALF HOURS ALLOWED

INSTRUCTIONS TO CANDIDATES

You have **TEN** minutes to read through this question paper before the start of the examination, during which time you may make notes on the examination paper.

IMPORTANT: *As soon as you receive this paper, read carefully the letter printed on page 4. Notes for a reply to this will be dictated to you as passage 2.*

Except where a different instruction is given, all letters should be typed on the headed paper provided, ready for signature as for despatch today. Where no special directions are given regarding display, any method, consistently used within each exercise, will be accepted.

Carbon copies should be taken only where indicated. Dictionaries and calculators may be used.

Candidates must satisfy the examiner in each section of the examination.

2

Passage 1
(5 marks)

An article of 150 words about Brighton and the south-east coast. To be typed in double (or 1½) line-spacing on plain white A4 paper. No heading is required.

Passage 2
(50 marks)

From the dictated notes, compose and type on plain white A4 paper a reply to the letter given on page 4. Type the appropriate letter-heading for this task.

Passage 3
(13 marks)

A memorandum from M Turner to Head of Bio-Engineering.

Passage 4
(25 marks)

A letter to Mr W North, 5 Church Lane, Exeter ER2 3EA. Our ref: DY/NC. One carbon copy on the yellow paper provided is required. Heading: FRANCHISES

Passage 5
(15 marks)

A letter to P T Thomas, 6 Sandalwood Avenue, Bromley, Kent BY3 7RH. Our ref: TB/MF. Heading: PRAXITELES SHARE GUIDE

Passage 6
(20 marks)

A report to be typed in double (or 1½) line-spacing on plain white A4 paper. Heading: INTERNATIONAL FOOD EXHIBITION

Passage 7
(12 marks)

A circular letter. Please leave at least 1½ inches (38 mm) for an address to be inserted later, and type DATE AS POSTMARK instead of today's date.

Passage 8
(60 marks)

A letter to The Manager, Praxi Bank plc, 120 Main Road, Mablethorpe, Lincs. Our ref: JB/wa. The Accounts referred to are printed on page 3 of this paper.

NB. *At the end of the examination you must insert all typewritten papers inside the cover of your answer book in the order of the examination paper and remain seated until this, together with the examination tape or disc, has been collected by the Invigilator.*

Accounts to accompany Passage 8   3

Trading and Profit and Loss Account } CAPS
for the year ended 24 February 1984

	£	£
Sales		306,150
(leave 1 clear line space)		
Purchases		264,090
(leave 1 clear line space)		
End stock – increase	–	
– decrease	2,870	
Cost of Sales		266,960
Gross Profit		39,190
(leave 1 clear line space)		
Bank charges	730	lc
Cleaning	900	trs
Hire purchase interest	510	uc
Insurances and licences	400	
Lighting and heating	1,470	
Motor expenses	1,340	lo
Postage, stationery and advertising	500	
Professional charges – accountancy	350	
– stocktaking	210	
Rates and water rates	2,980	
Repairs and renewals – property	–	
– general	1,600	
Sundry trade expenses		310
Telephone	310	
Wages and National Insurance	20,660	
Wrapping paper	370	
Overhead expenses		32,650
		6,540
Depreciation :–		
(leave 1 clear line space)		
Furniture and Fittings	740	
Refrigerator	200	
Bacon slicer	170	
Motor vehicles	2,880	
		3,990
Net Profit for the year		£2,550

4

Letter for reply — Passage 2

9145 South Damen
Chicago
Illinois IL 60202
United States of America

24 April 1984

The Manager
Norfolk Estate Agents
20 College Road
Norwich
England

Dear Sir

We are looking for some temporary accommodation for approximately 9 months from October 1984 to June 1985, as we are returning to England for a long vacation, and would like to spend some time in the Norwich area.

Ideally we would like a small 3-bedroomed house with central heating near to the town as we will not have a car.

We look forward to hearing from you.

Yours faithfully

E. Parsons

E Parsons (Mrs)

Model Tasks

The following section contains model tasks for all the numbered tasks. Model tasks for the Production tasks appear in the Teacher's Book.

UNIT 1

Task 1:1

We thank you for your order for our products.

We regret that we have completely sold out.

There was a very heavy demand for these goods.

Our workers were on overtime for several months.

We hope to despatch your order next week.

Task 1:2

We have just received your letter with enclosures.

We are very pleased with the new designs.

We think these will appeal to our younger customers.

We shall forward the designs to our branches.

We hope to place our order in due course.

Task 1:3

We would like you to study the enclosed literature.

Full details of our latest range are given.

These products are offered at very good discounts.

There is a good market for these products locally.

Please let us know if you are interested.

Task 1:4

Thank you for your recent letter with enclosed order.

We are sorry to say we no longer manufacture these goods.

We now make a product of slightly different design.

We are enclosing some leaflets for your attention.

We look forward to hearing further from you.

UNIT 2   Task 2:1

We have received your request concerning colour televisions and are enclosing full details.

You will notice that our cheapest model is good value when compared with those of our competitors.

At the other end of the list is our luxury model which is superior to any other on the market.

We think your customers will like our sets as we have the best range on offer.

We look forward to hearing from you and hope that you will place a trial order.

Task 2:2

Thank you for your enquiry concerning holidays abroad for which I am enclosing brochures.

This year we have a variety of holidays which we are sure will interest you.

You may like a sunny holiday on the coast or perhaps a quiet rest in pleasant surroundings.

Our brochure lists only the very best hotels at which you can be sure of good service.

You should return the booking form immediately to make sure you are not disappointed.

Task 2:3

Thank you for your recent letter and for returning your copy of the inventory.

We are pleased to hear that you enjoyed your holiday and that the caravan was in a good location.

We are refunding your deposit with an additional amount to pay for the broken chair.

We agree that the chair needed replacing and that you are not responsible for the extra charge.

We look forward to receiving a booking from you for next year and will send you the new brochure soon.

Task 2:4

Thank you for your order for our kitchen equipment which will be despatched during the next few days

We do not have any storage jars in stock at the moment and we will send these to you as soon as possible.

We can give you a refund for these goods immediately if you prefer not to wait.

We are enclosing our new catalogue and price list from which you will see that some new lines are available.

We are pleased to say that most of our our goods cost the same price as that charged last year.

UNIT 3

Task 3:1

I was very interested to hear of the book which you are writing about your childhood. I am sure that the public will be very interested in the life of such a famous sportsman.

I should like to have a meeting with you to discuss the book. We could either meet at my office in town or at your home in the country. Please let me know which you prefer.

I very much look forward to meeting you. I should be grateful if you would telephone me to arrange a suitable time and date. I look forward to hearing further from you.

Task 3:2

I shall write to Mr John Brown and thank him for his letter. He wrote saying that he could not attend the interview next Tuesday. He can come at the same time on Thursday.

I think we should hold the interview at our new offices in Oxford Street. It will be easy for Mr Brown to get there as he lives in Harrow. He will be able to travel in by car or on the underground.

Mr Brown will work at our Birmingham factory if he is appointed. It is important to point this out to Mr Brown at the interview. He may not wish to move so far if he has children of school age.

Task 3:3

We have written to Mr K Smith to invite him to a meeting of our Sales Representatives. The meeting will be held in the Board Room on Friday next. Lunch will be served before the meeting.

Mr Smith used to work for a large American firm at their London office. The position he held was International Sales Director of the Company. He will therefore have much to say of value to our Sales Representatives.

We hope Mr Smith can advise us on the introduction of our new product to the British market. We do not think he is interested in a permanent job in this country. We might consider appointing him as a Consultant to our Company.

Task 3:4

We have received a brochure from the local travel agency and are interested in flights to the United States. We are not yet sure whether it would be best to fly to New York or Washington.

It is not clear from the literature which airports are used by these flights and we wonder whether they are from Gatwick or Heathrow. It would be easier for us to get to Gatwick Airport as we live in Brighton.

When we are in America we would like to hire a car. We understand that it is easy to do this with companies such as Avis and Hertz. Can you confirm that the booking and payment can be made here and the car collected from the airport in the States?

UNIT 4

Task 4:1

We have heard from our suppliers in Hong Kong that several cargoes of radios should reach us in January. These are packed in cardboard boxes with a dozen in each of the crates.

In addition to the radios there will be a consignment of quartz watches. These come in several styles for both men and women. There is also a range for children which feature pictures of their latest screen heroes on the watch faces.

We are only one of several companies importing these goods. We think that the prices are excellent and that they will sell throughout the cities and counties of the UK without difficulty. There will be no exclusive agencies for these products.

Task 4:2

We are interested in purchasing some new word processors which your Company is marketing. We would like further information on the complete range of models.

Can you ask one of your Sales Representatives to call. It would be best if he telephoned my Secretary first to make a firm appointment.

We are looking for models which will be easy to operate and which our secretaries can learn to use without difficulty. We notice that you supply machines made by firms such as Wang and IBM. We now believe we should be replacing all our electric typewriters with word processors or electronic machines.

Task 4:3

The number of women senior directors in most businesses is usually very small. Most women directors are traditionally found in the area of personnel management. Probably the best way for women to get into senior management is through obtaining university degrees or professional qualifications.

Many graduates wanting to get into business will find that it is worthwhile to obtain secretarial qualifications. This is particularly true if careers in the publishing industry or the media are of interest.

Secretarial skills are undoubtedly useful in themselves. The ability to type accurately and quickly is a real asset when using computers. A good knowledge of office systems and equipment is also very useful. Shorthand can be of considerable benefit in meetings and when drafting reports. Many women managers who have progressed from secretarial positions value their secretarial skills highly.

UNIT 5

Task 5:1

Thank you for your recent letter enclosing your order for cottons, silks and woollen fabrics. Unfortunately(,) we are out of stock of the cottons you require but our Purchasing Manager, Mr A North, expects delivery next week.

Referring to your previous order, the goods were despatched by fast, reliable, delivery van. Please confirm in writing whether this method of delivery is satisfactory. If there are problems(,) we shall do our best to solve them.

Mr John Jackson, our representative for the North West Area, will call to see you within the next week. We hope you will place orders for nylon, rayon, terylene and other synthetics for your summer styles.

Task 5:2

The Financial Director of our Company, Mrs Janice Roberts, started with the firm as a secretary. She was eventually promoted to Personal Assistant to the Managing Director. She studied accountancy at evening classes, passing her examinations in record time. Mrs Roberts then took up the post of Accounts Manager in 1981(,) and was eventually invited to be the Financial Director on the retirement of Mr James Gordon.

Mrs Roberts is an excellent example to other women in the Company who wish to progress from secretarial work to management posts.

When interviewed by the local newspaper, Mrs Roberts said that the hard work had been worthwhile. The most difficult time, she agreed, was when her son, now three years old, was a tiny baby. She said it was important that those women who desired to succeed in their chosen careers were firmly established in their jobs before taking time off to start a family.

Task 5:3

It is true that Christmas comes only once a year(,) but many businesses depend upon this one important day. In the few weeks before Christmas, many manufacturers achieve as much as half of their total sales. This is true of greeting card manufacturers, manufacturers of novelties and decorations, and even some food producers. Christmas, despite what many people would rather believe, really is big business.

In fact(,) Christmas existed in the form of a winter feast long before the religion which now gives it a name. All European societies, it seems, felt the need for a cheerful holiday in the middle of the long, dark, cold winter days.

So businessmen should not feel too guilty if the true spirit of Christmas sometimes seems to be lacking from their activities. Mr Roy Charles, a Director of a famous London store, told businessmen at a conference recently(,) that they should keep up the good work of meeting the needs and wishes of the consumer at Christmas. Many jobs, in addition to much happiness, depend on it.

Task 6:1

MW/BB

Date

Mrs C Thompson
23 Dorset Gardens
Bournemouth
BH2 1NH

Dear Mrs Thompson

Thank you for your recent enquiry about a portable typewriter for your own use. We have several excellent models in stock, including electronic machines. We suggest you call in at our shop to inspect the full range.

During next month this Branch will be holding its annual sale. If you do not require the typewriter urgently, it would be to your advantage to wait. The prices of current models will be drastically reduced. Since you have placed orders with us in the past, we should like you to have the benefit of a price reduction.

Yours sincerely

Michael Woods
MANAGER

Task 6:2

MEM/2371

Date

Mr C Hatchard BA
15 Royal Court
Hayards Ave
Watford
WD3 6QR

Dear Sir

MEMBERSHIP OF THE SOCIETY

In response to your recent request, I enclose a booklet which gives details of Membership of the Society, together with an application form. When you have completed the form you should return it to me, enclosing the registration fee.

If you do not possess the necessary educational qualifications you will be able to sit an entry examination next July. Your attention is drawn to the Examination Rules in the booklet.

I look forward to hearing further from you.

Yours faithfully

Secretary

Encs

UNIT 6

Task 6:3

Date

Mr and Mrs D Piper
62 Spring Street
LONDON
N1 4AN

Dear Mr and Mrs Piper

Thank you for your completed Mortgage Application Form. I am pleased to say that an advance will be made during the next few weeks.

We have written to your solicitor today confirming that the mortgage application was successful. We have asked her to let us know the date of Exchange of Contracts as soon as possible, so that the overdraft facility to cover the deposit can be made available.

We are now enclosing life assurance application forms for you both to complete and return.

Yours sincerely

Manager

Encs

UNIT 7

Task 7:1

DK/--

Date

Mrs E Small MP
Constituency Headquarters
Bridge Road
LONDON
SW18 4JB

Dear Mrs Small

I am writing to confirm our telephone conversation this morning and the
arrangements for the visit to the Houses of Parliament by a party of our
students on Thursday next. These students are studying government in
connection with their course in business studies. As mentioned, they
should arrive at 1430 hrs: there will be 40 students and 2 lecturers. It
is really very kind of you to conduct the tour personally, and I am sure
the afternoon will be both interesting and enjoyable.

May I call on your help in another way? The College is taking as its theme
for Open Day next term ´European Britain´ and the idea behind this is to
show the effects of Common Market membership on British life. As I know
that you are very interested in the EEC, I wonder whether you would come
and talk to our students on a topic related to this theme. The date of
Open Day could be arranged to suit your convenience since you would be the
main guest speaker.

I look forward to hearing from you and should like to thank you for the
interest you show in the College.

Your sincerely

David Kennedy
PRINCIPAL

UNIT 7

Task 7:2

10 Charlotte Square

Ramsgate

Kent

CT11 9HJ

Date

RG/--

The Manager
Universal Appliances Ltd
Endsleigh House
London   W6 8HH

Dear Sir

SUPER WASHING MACHINE MODEL NO 31

I purchased one of your washing machines one month ago from the department store here in Ramsgate. Since then it has given considerable trouble.

The first time the machine was used it operated perfectly. However, the second time it was used water flooded all over the floor. I telephoned your office and was told that one of your repair men would call the next afternoon - he did not. He did, however, call the following morning when we were out. My wife made 2 subsequent appointments for the repair man to call and was let down on both occasions. Eventually, when he did keep the appointment, the repair man found that the machine needed a minor part which he did not have with him. The part was fitted only yesterday, after yet another broken appointment.

I really must complain about this lack of service. I believed that I was buying a machine from a firm with a first-class service; unfortunately, this was not true. I should appreciate your comments.

Yours faithfully

Robert Grant

UNIT 7

Household Products Limited

27-29 Chester Road

DARLINGTON   CO.DURHAM

DL1 8GG

Our ref   Sales/23/PLJ
Your ref WP/MM

Date

Northern Wholesalers Ltd
180 Great Western Way
Manchester
M1 2DG

FOR THE ATTN OF MR W PRICE

Dear Sirs

ORDER NO B.249

We have received your recent letter complaining about the poor condition of the china and crockery items which we delivered to you recently. We have investigated the matter and found that the order form which we received from you had not been completed correctly.

The form states that you should 'Indicate the method of delivery by striking through 2 of the following: road/rail/delivery van'. As your order was fragile we think it should have been sent by delivery van. You will note that in the Conditions printed on the reverse side of the order form, it is clearly stated that our Company cannot be held liable for breakages of fragile items in transit <u>unless</u> the goods are despatched by delivery van. Unfortunately, whoever filled in the order form in your office asked for delivery by rail.

In the circumstances, therefore, we regret that we are unable to compensate you for the broken and cracked items.

Yours faithfully
HOUSEHOLD PRODUCTS LIMITED

P L Jones

UNIT 8

Task 8:1

MEMO

To   Sales Manager   Ref   MS/EF
From   Accounts Manager   Date

GRICE AND SONS LTD

Would you please note that the above Company are now above their credit limit. I have heard from several business associates that this firm has been having a very difficult time lately. In the circumstances I think no further orders should be accepted from them until the major part of their balance is cleared.

Since you have good contacts with this firm I should be grateful if you would write them a tactful letter.

Task 8:2

                          MEMORANDUM

TO: Manchester Office   REF: LW/PP

FROM: Head Office, London   DATE: (Today´s)

HEADING: Stationery Supplies

At a recent meeting here, it was decided that all stationery supplies are to be purchased from Office Suppliers Limited, since an exceptionally large discount has been granted for bulk quantities.

It is important that you conform with Company policy on this matter, as failure by any branch to order from Office Suppliers may result in the Company not purchasing a total quantity sufficient to obtain this discount.

It is understood that your own local supplier can quote prices below those of Office Suppliers, but in this case your raised costs will be offset by savings at other branches throughout the country. Would you please ensure that all further orders for stationery are sent to: The Purchasing Manager, Office Suppliers Limited, 10 Green Lane, London, N4 8QQ.

UNIT 8

Task 8:3

ACCTS/LQ/--

Date

Mr R Richardson
25 Regent St
Wolverhampton
WV2 4DB

Dear Sir

ACCOUNT NO 31799

It is with regret that we must draw your attention to the fact that your account with our Company is now considerably overdue.

Under the terms of the Agreement you guaranteed to pay £15.31 per month, or 10% of the outstanding balance - whichever figure is the smaller. Your arrears now total £45.93. We should appreciate payment by return of post.

Yours faithfully
REGAL STORES LIMITED

Accounts Manager

UNIT 8

Task 8:4

MEMO

To   General Manager   Ref   PERS/LE/KK

From   Staff Manager   Date

CAR PARKING

I am writing to you to report on the meeting with the Works Committee
yesterday evening, in view of the fact that I am going on holiday tomorrow,
and have been unable to contact you all the afternoon.

The main problem that was discussed was the question of car parking.
Whilst it is appreciated that parking space at the factory is somewhat
limited, the shop-floor workers complained about the system by which spaces
are allocated. They accept that all senior managers should have reserved
places in the car park, but they want the remaining spaces given out on a
different basis than at present. At the moment spaces are awarded on the
basis of seniority in the Company. However, in practice this has meant
that office staff have had priority over shop-floor workers. It was felt
by most workers present that there was no justification for allocating
space to every new manager or secretary rather than to a long-serving
production worker. It was suggested therefore that spaces be allocated on
the basis of years of service with the Company.

Something must be done fairly soon as there is a strong feeling of
resentment because some new, young typists have been given spaces recently.

My own feeling is that we should get the new car park ready earlier than
originally planned and, in the meantime, adopt the scheme proposed by the
production workers for any further allocations.

I shall be back in the office on Monday fortnight.

UNIT 8

Task 8:5

JH/--

Date

Mr L Kimpton
48 North Street
Coventry
CV1 5RS

Dear Mr Kimpton

Thank you for your recent letter. I enclose the BA and British Caledonian timetables you requested. Both airlines have flights to Spain.

I have investigated your complaint about the service on board a recent flight from Tangier to London. The Public Relations Officer for the airline states that the flight on which you travelled home should have called at Gibraltar on the way to Tangier. However, the plane could not land at Gibraltar because of gale force winds: the runway there is very short. Thus the fresh food and drinks ordered there were not, of course, taken on board, and the Chief Stewardess had to get emergency supplies at Tangier. These supplies were not up to the usual high standards of the airline.

I trust this explanation is acceptable and look forward to receiving your booking for your forthcoming trip to Spain.

Yours sincerely

John Hopkins
MANAGER

Enc

UNIT 9

Task 9:1

JOHN CONSTABLE AND COMPANY LIMITED

The Company's Annual General Meeting was held at the offices in Green Street, Glasgow, on 21st March. The Chairman's statement had been previously circulated.

The year's results were fairly good considering strong competition from abroad. Some new lines had to be sold at uneconomic prices, and this did not help the Company's profits. Many companies' accounts showed decreased dividends similar to Constable's. The Chairman remarked that an encouraging fact was that competitors' results were less satisfactory.

The Chairman thanked the Directors for their hard work and pointed out that they depend to a large extent on the staff's loyalty. A vote of thanks was proposed by one of the shareholders and unanimously approved.

UNIT 9

Task 9:2

MEMO

To   All Departmental Managers   Ref

From Personnel Manager   Date

CONDITIONS OF SERVICE

You are reminded of the following points concerning the above:

1   The hours of work at the Company´s offices are 9 am to 5 pm. The
     hours of work at the Company´s factories are 8 am to 5.30 pm.

2   Directors, managers and employees with 3 years´ experience of
     working for the Company are entitled to contribute to the Pension
     Fund.

3   All employees of the Company are entitled to 3 weeks´ annual holiday:
     employees who have worked for 5 years qualify for an extra week´s
     holiday.

4   Company cars are provided for all managers. The firm´s cars are
     not to be used for any individual´s private business. Directors´
     cars may be parked in the reserved car park.

5   It is each manager´s responsibility to ensure his staff arrive
     punctually, and to report any employee´s absence.

UNIT 9

Task 9:3

JJ/QWM

Date

Mrs P Josephs
16 Watford Way
Kingston-upon-Thames
Surrey   KT4 3DS

Dear Mrs Josephs

I am pleased to say that your case will come before the Court within the next few weeks. The correspondence has already been forwarded to the Queen's Counsel, who will advise on the main points of law. He will study the draft document, which states the principles raised by the case. The Q.C. will then send us his opinion, trying to elicit the main points of disagreement in the dispute.

I enclose a draft letter to the defendant for you to check, which states our principal objections to his claims. When you have had the opportunity to study the draft, please ensure that you return it to me as soon as possible. We shall see what effect this has!

Yours sincerely

Enc

UNIT 9

Task 9:4

MEMO

To   Foreman   Ref   KT/MP

From Site Manager   Date

KING STREET SITE

Would you please note that work on the new site will commence next Monday morning, weather permitting. The licence has now been received from the town council. Would you please hire 4 additional labourers for this important job.

We are very short of both lead pipes and steel tubes, and will need to take delivery of a further supply as soon as possible. The last load was left under canvas on the site and has disappeared. The police advise us to make better arrangements to ensure we do not lose it this time - there are many people who will steal lead for its value sold as scrap. Unfortunately we are unable to insure ourselves against this type of loss.

UNIT 10

Task 10:1

<u>DRAFT</u>

Dear Mr Wilson

ABRAHAM AND COMPANY LIMITED

Further to your recent letter, we have made the necessary enquiries concerning the above company. The partners in the business are Mr S Abraham and Mr R Rice. The company manufactures leather goods on a small scale and sells direct to retail outlets. Mr Rice has a record of business failure – a company which he managed and owned went bankrupt 7 years ago. It appears that one of his partners was taking too much cash out of the business and eventually had to serve a term in prison. Obviously, this failure was due mainly to circumstances beyond the control of Mr Rice. Our informants tell us that the personal reputation of Mr Rice is sound.

However, in the circumstances, it may be best to be cautious. We suggest that at least the first few orders be accepted on a cash-with-order basis. If you subsequently decide to grant a credit limit to this company, we think it should be at the minimum level consistent with the maintenance of good business relationships.

We trust the above information is of service to you, and assure you of our strictest confidence.

Yours sincerely

UNIT 10

Task 10:2

Date as Postmark

Dear Sir/Madam

You will be interested to hear that we have recently brought out a new range of cosmetics which we are sure you will want to market. This complete range of beauty products is designed for the 13 to 19 age group and is attractively packaged in bright yellow containers. We are enclosing fully descriptive literature and a price list.

Our Representative will call on you in the very near future to deliver a special display cabinet for use with these products. As an introductory offer, we will allow a 20% discount on goods purchased within the next 3 months.

We look forward to receiving your order in the near future.

Yours faithfully
SUSAN SMITH PRODUCTS

Sales Manager

Encs

UNIT 10

Task 10:3

STAFF NOTICE

Coffee and Tea Breaks

The canteen is becoming very crowded each morning at approximately eleven o'clock and long queues have been forming at the counters. It would be of considerable help if staff could try to stagger their breaks over a longer period, and avoid crowding in the middle of the morning.

It has also been noticed that some staff are taking considerably longer than the 15 minutes allowed for tea and coffee breaks. Because some staff are sitting at tables too long, others arriving later cannot find seats in the canteen. Please leave the canteen after 15 minutes to avoid causing this congestion.

It is hoped that staff will voluntarily take action to reduce pressure on the canteen facilities. If there is no improvement, however, management will have to take steps to ensure that breaks are more strictly regulated.

STAFF MANAGER

UNIT 10

Task 10:4

COMMUNITY ARTS FESTIVAL

The Community Arts Festival in East London was the scene last week of a variety of activities reflecting the great richness of the many cultures of people in this multi-ethnic community.

Among the events featured was a beautiful display of traditional dances performed by members of the Asian communities, when the wonderful colours and fabrics of costumes were also much admired.

The West Indian community organized a lively carnival, accompanied by the music of steel bands. Everyone joined in this with much enthusiasm.

English cultural tradition was represented by a range of traditional and modern plays at the local theatre. Highlight of the week was the party to which each ethnic group contributed typical food and delicacies.

UNIT 11

Part I

EARLY NOVELS OF GREAT BRITISH WRITERS - CONTINUED

All in hardback at £1 each (post and packing extra)

Please use the order form on page 15

VIVIAN GREY   DISRAELI, BENJAMIN (1804-1881)

His plan to create a new political party fails and after a duel he leaves for adventures in Europe.

MARY BARTON   GASKELL, Elizabeth Cleghorn (1810-1865)

Mary's admirer is shot dead. Her lover is accused and tried; she desperately strives to save him.

VANITY FAIR   THACKERAY, William Makepeace (1811-1863)

The contrasting life-stories of two girls: Becky Sharp is hard and clever but poor, whereas Amelia Sedley is gentle, dull and rich.

OLIVER TWIST   DICKENS, Charles (1812-1870)

The story of a boy, born in a workhouse, who runs away to London and falls in with a gang of thieves.

Page 5

UNIT 11

Part II — Passage 1

Dear Sir/Madam

Everyone interested in books is aware that prices are very high. Many
people would like to own more books but cannot afford to buy them because
of the increased cost of living.

We have decided to offer, at bargain prices, a number of recently published
books and a selection from previous lists. A copy of our sale catalogue is
enclosed. This offer is open until the end of July, 1983, and applies only
to the United Kingdom. Payment can be made by cheque, National Giro,
Barclaycard or Access. If your order comes to more than £20, you may
choose a book from the free gift page.

A word of warning! Some of the titles offered are in limited supply. If
there is one which you would particularly like to own, please send for it
immediately - you may be disappointed if you delay.

We hope that you will benefit from our sale. Should you know of anyone
else who would be interested in our offer, please ask them to write to us
for a catalogue.

Yours truly

Encs

UNIT 11

Part II — Passage 2

SITE SAFETY '83 - CONSTRUCTION SAFETY EXHIBITION

The aim of the safety year is to reduce the high level of accidents in the Construction Industry. Many workers take unnecessary risks. Most accidents that happen could, and should, be prevented.

A safety exhibition, open from 10 am until 8 pm, will be held at the Technical College on Wednesday, Thursday and Friday of next week. Admission will be free.

The directors of our firm wish all employees to visit the exhibition and particularly to see the excellent training films which will run continuously. Arrangements have been made for everyone to go during working hours (without loss of pay). Your supervisor will tell you when your coach will leave.

S Christopher
SAFETY OFFICER

Date

UNIT 11

Part II — Passage 3

AS/883

2 March 1983

Henderson & James Ltd
23 St Anne's Square
HITCHIN
Herts
SG5 1QB

Dear Sirs

CLARKE LIMITED - ADVERTISING SUPPLEMENT

On 15 June, Clarke Limited, the well-known office equipment firm, will open an extension to their London showrooms. In that week's issue of our newspaper we shall include a special article contained in a four-page supplement announcing this important event.

We understand that you have supplied them with office sundries for many years. You are invited to insert in this supplement an advertisement linking your firm and its products with Clarke Limited. We are offering a discount of 20% off our usual charges.

Over the last 2 years we have printed several of these supplements. Most firms who have taken up our offer say that they consider improvements in their sales were largely due to this particular form of advertising.

Some samples of advertisements (with prices) and an order form are enclosed. Please telephone if you require further information.

Yours faithfully

Encs

UNIT 11

Part II — Passage 4

MEMORANDUM

To   Managing Director   Ref
From Office Manager   Date 2 March 1983

PORTABLE CABIN FOR TEMPORARY OFFICE ACCOMMODATION

Our new offices will be ready by late November. We had thought that we could manage with the space available until then. However, our business is expanding so quickly that we must have more room now.

We could easily stand a portable cabin against the west wall of the office block. The audio-typists could occupy it; their present accommodation could be used by the accounts department.

Hiring a cabin would be better than buying - it would be needed for only a few months. The cost would be the hiring charge less the tax saved.

Some illustrated brochures are attached; I have marked the cabin which I consider would be most suitable. Please let me have your comments soon.

Encs

UNIT 13

Task 13:1

Month, Year

Dear Member

This year's bonus offer of music cassettes
in the classical section of the Club's
list, is the following 3 symphonies
recently recorded by the London Festival
Orchestra:

Beethoven	Symphony No 6		'Pastoral'
Mozart	"	" 38	'Prague'
Schubert	"	" 8	'Unfinished'

For this special bonus offer cassettes are
priced £2.75 each, or £7 for the set.
This offer is open until the end of next
month, and the order form is enclosed.

Yours sincerely
CASSETTE MUSIC LIMITED

Enc

UNIT 13

Task 13:2

JM/--

Date

Mr L Machin
18 Vera Way
Harlow
Essex
CM19 5BN

Dear Mr Machin

Further to your visit to our Agency yesterday when we discussed
Italian Tour No 78 in our brochure, we have pleasure in
informing you that we have provisionally reserved the following
accommodation for you:

Week beginning 18 July - one double room with bath at the Park
Hotel in Rome

Week beginning 25 July - one twin-bedded room at the Hotel Maria
in Naples

We confirm that the price as advertised includes all travel from
the West London Air Terminal to the first hotel, between the hotels,
and return. If you wish to secure this booking, a deposit of £10
per person is required within the next 10 days. This can be paid
by cheque or in cash at the Agency.

I look forward to hearing further from you.

Yours sincerely

John Martin
MANAGER

UNIT 13

Task 13:3

MEMO

To   Staff   Ref

From   Personnel Manager   Date

ANNUAL DINNER AND DANCE

The Annual Dinner and Dance will take place at the Swan Hotel on 12 June at 7.30 pm. Tickets will be available during the preceding fortnight, on sale in the Accounts Department. Tickets cost £7 double and £4 single. After discussion, the Staff Committee selected the following simple menu which it was felt would appeal to most people:

Tomato Soup
or
Chilled Melon

Roast Pork with Stuffing
or Grilled Lamb Cutlets
Roast and Creamed Potatoes
Cauliflower, Carrots and Green Beans

Fresh Fruit Salad and Cream
or Sherry Trifle

Cheese and Biscuits

Coffee

It is hoped that the dinner will prove to be as great a success as in previous years. Dancing will be to the Latin Trio and a mobile discotheque. The cabaret will include entertainment from the comedian, Eric Peters.

UNIT 13

Task 13:4

JKR/HJ/--

Date

Mr V Graham
6 Willow Court
5-8 Gloucester Road
Exeter
Devon   EX5 4NU

Dear Sir

Further to my visit to the block of flats at 5-8 Gloucester Road, I have
pleasure in quoting my Company's price for the interior decoration of
the staircases and communal entrance halls, and for the painting of the
exterior woodwork. The quotation is as follows:

Decoration of staircases and all external woodwork	£2,200
Replastering of water-damaged walls in main hall	160
Painting of concrete sections between exterior brickwork (if required)	190
	£3,500

Plus VAT at 15%

I confirm that 6 men will be employed on this job and that the work
can start in approximately 3 months' time. If this quotation is acceptable, I shall deliver paint colour charts immediately so that the Residents
Committee may make their choice. This will ensure that the paint is
ordered and delivered well before the work is due to commence.

I assure you of our prompt and reliable attention at all times.

Yours faithfully
RUGBY BUILDERS LIMITED

John K Rugby
DIRECTOR

UNIT 14

Task 14:1

EXCEL GARAGE DOORS

EXCEL garage doors are made to measure garage doors. There is therefore no need to adhere to standard opening sizes when building new garages. Nor is there any necessity to convert an existing opening to a standard door size when replacing old doors. EXCEL up-and-over doors are made to measure doors at the same prices as for standard doors. They incorporate the best principles of overhead door design, and require the minimum of space and maintenance.

The up-and-over door mechanism is of robust construction. The door is securely held in the raised position, yet is gently lowered at a touch. There are several design specifications available.

The MODERN up-and-over door combines the best features of both aluminimum and steel. The welded steel frame is coated after assembly with a rustproofed zinc finish, suitable for painting. It provides a sturdy framework that will withstand heavy and constant use. The aluminium panels are strong, weather-resisting, and have an attractive finish. The MODERN garage door is exceptionally good value and is the cheapest of our range.

TRADITIONAL up-and-over doors can be styled in either Georgian or Tudor design. They are constructed of either black or white coloured glass fibre. The Tudor style door has a simulated wood grain finish.

The COUNTRY up-and-over door is also made of glass fibre. This has a wood grain finish but is designed in a way which will blend with any house style.

There is no difference in the cost of TRADITIONAL and COUNTRY up-and-over garage doors.

UNIT 14

Table for 14.1

EXCEL GARAGE DOORS

TYPE	OPENING SIZE				
	Height		Weight		Max Thickness
	Min	Max	Min	Max	
MODERN	1740 mm (5'9½'')	2134 mm (7'0'')	27 kg (60 lb)	36 kg (80 lb)	51 mm (2'')
TRADITIONAL	1784 mm (5'10¼'')	2134 mm (7'0'')	27 kg (60 lb)	59 kg (130 lb)	51 mm (2'')
COUNTRY	1784 mm (5'10¼'')	2286 mm (7'6'')	59 kg (130 lb)	91 kg (200 lb)	57 mm (2¼'')

Note: For extreme ease of operation, and particularly by a short person, we recommend that the door height does not exceed 1981 mm (6'6'').

UNIT 14

Task 14:2

Date

Mrs A D Street
Westcliff College of Commerce
Straight Road
Westcliff-on-Sea
Essex   SSO 9LD

Dear Madam

STATEMENT NO J2322

Thank you for your recent letter. In order to clarify the position for you
I set out below details of the items shown on your statement for last month:

Order No	Quantity	Title and Author	Unit Price £	Total Price £
1641	50	Economic Theory by P W Bellamy	**2.00**	100.00
1653	30	Accounts and Auditing Practice by M S Chesterton	2.10	63.00
1666	18	Computer Programming Made Easy by Mary Green	4.80	86.40
"	10	Management Techniques by Paul Grey	1.50	15.00
"	15	Industrial Sociology by M M McKay	4.00	60.00
				324.40
LESS 1631	50	Business Economics by P W Bellamy	1.60	80.00
				£244.40

It seems that the confusion has arisen over the return of 50 books by
Bellamy and the purchase of 50 of a different title by the same author,
but at a <u>higher</u> price.

UNIT 14

2

Date

Mrs A D Street

We trust that this clarifies the situation for you and look forward to receiving your cheque in settlement in due course. As you can see, the outstanding amount is £244.40.

Yours faithfully

UNIT 14

Task 14:3

Constituency Headquarters
Bridge Road
LONDON
SW18 4JB

Your ref DK/--
Our ref ES/--

Date

Mr D Kennedy MA
South Thames College
River Hill
London   SW15 4KJ

Dear Mr Kennedy

Thank you for your letter of yesterday's date. I confirm the arrangements detailed in your letter, and very much look forward to meeting the party from the College next Thursday.

I should be very pleased to attend the College Open Day and speak to the students. I suggest as the title of my talk 'The Political Consequences of Britain's Entry', as this is the aspect of EEC membership which most interests me. I am able to come to the College on any Friday afternoon, as I keep this time free for work in the Constituency. Thus, if Open Day is held on a Friday next term, I shall be very pleased to attend.

If this suggestion is suitable, please let me know the exact date as soon as possible so that I can refuse any further invitations or engagements. I look forward to hearing further from you.

Yours sincerely

Mrs E Small

UNIT 14

Task 14:4

NORTHERN WHOLESALERS LIMITED
180 Great Western Way
MANCHESTER
M1 2DG

Your ref Sales/32/PLJ
Our ref WP/MM

Date

FOR THE ATTN OF MR P L JONES

Household Products Ltd
27-29 Chester Road
Darlington
Co Durham
DL1 8GG

Dear Sirs

ORDER NO B.249

We have received your letter of yesterday's date and agree that the damage to the goods resulted from an error in the completion of the form. We apologise for our original complaint. We will of course investigate the matter and ensure that all future orders for fragile goods request delivery by van.

However, we think that it would be helpful to your customers if this important instruction were printed on the front of the order form, rather than in the small print on the back, where it can be easily overlooked.

We are enclosing our order form for the replacement of the broken and cracked items, together with our cheque in settlement.

Would you also please send us your latest catalogue and price lists.

Yours faithfully
NORTHERN WHOLESALERS LTD

W PRICE

Encs

UNIT 15

Passage 1

Public relations in its many forms is vital to all institutions whether
they be trade associations, professional bodies, or research organisations.

There is a need to tell the public at large, as well as your own members
about your work.   Possible new members and consumers at home and abroad,
as well as employees and other interested persons, need to be kept
informed, and each may need a different style of approach.   Your internal
news sheet will not be suitable for the general public, and neither will
your annual report.

A successful public relations programme does not just happen.   It has to be
planned and followed up professionally, just as the budget planning and
control programme would be.   When institutes want reliable financial advice
they go to the expert, namely their accountant.   Does this happen to
anything like the same extent when it comes to their very important public
relations strategy?

UNIT 15

Passage 2

21 June 1983

London Books PLC
Subscriptions Department
8 The Leathermarket
LONDON
SE1 2EB

Dear Sirs

Thank you for your enquiry of 10 June, requesting details of our publications available to the general public.

I enclose a leaflet giving details of all our current publications, together with prices. You will note that booksellers are allowed a trade discount of 15%.

We shall be pleased to supply you with any of these publications on receipt of a completed order form.

Yours faithfully

Pamela Thrush
SECRETARY TO PUBLICATIONS MANAGER

Enc

UNIT 15

passage 2 contd)

<u>BTRA - Publications</u>

Price to
Members*

<u>BTRA Conference Books</u>

(A4 bound papers)

The Working Environment in Materials Manufacturing Industries, 282 pp	£25.75
Materials Technology for the '80s, 370 pp	£30.00

<u>Booklets</u>

Behaviour of Materials under Stress	£ 1.00
Quality Means Business	£ 1.50
Engineering Data on Materials (SI Units)	£ 1.50
(Imperial Units)	£ 1.00

<u>Broadsheets</u>

Technical information sheets - 200 titles available - please send for full list	
Sets of 25 Broadsheets in ready-bound covers	£ 5.00
Individual Broadsheets	50p each

<u>Periodicals</u>

Abstracts of International Materials Literature (published bi-monthly) Annual subscription payable in advance (6 issues plus index)	£40.00

* Non-members
add 75%

Please note zero rate VAT on all publications

All prices include packing and postage

Trade discount of 15% to booksellers

UNIT 15

Passage 3

Our ref LS/PT
Your ref JC/22

21 June 1983

Miss Janet Cooper
American Technical Publications Corporation
PO Box 2550
88 Bedford Square
LONDON   WC1B 3FH

Dear Miss Cooper

Thank you for your letter of 9 June which followed a note in the February
issue of "Modern Materials" about our periodical "Abstracts of
International Materials Literature". I have pleasure in enclosing details
of the volume produced during 1982, and also that being produced during the
current year.

"Abstracts" is produced as a result of searching technical publications
from world-wide sources and the scope of "Abstracts" is being progressively
widened to include an increasing number of items on plastics.

I also enclose leaflets about our other publications, including technical
information broadsheets, conference report books, and translations. These
latter are available only to member companies, but we should be delighted
to enrol your organisation as an associate member if you so wish, and I
enclose details of our associate membership arrangements.

Yours sincerely

Publications Manager

Encs

UNIT 15

Passage 4

21 June 1983

AIRMAIL

Mr V Godjal
Laine (PVT) Ltd
Padi
MADRAS
India
600 001

Dear Sir

Thank you for your letter of 2 June. We are pleased to note your interest in our booklet on Engineering Data on Materials. This is available in both SI and Imperial Units, but can only be supplied on a sale basis. A leaflet is enclosed giving details.

We regret that we can only supply publications to addresses overseas on receipt of the appropriate remittance, and we are therefore also enclosing our pro forma invoice to cover the supply of one each of the booklets. The prices given in the leaflet cover postage and packing by surface mail, but as we have had repeated problems with items sent by surface mail failing to arrive at their destination in India, we have taken the liberty of adding an air mail charge as we find this a more reliable service.

If we can be of any further assistance, please let us know.

Yours faithfully

Enc

UNIT 15

Passage 5

21 June 1983

Mr James Findlay
Findlay & Baker Ltd
707 Retford Road
SHEFFIELD
S1 3WH

Dear Sir

Thank you for your letter concerning translations of papers appearing in the foreign language technical press.

We only commission translations of papers which we think will be of general interest to our members, and a list of those currently available is enclosed. If any member company requests a translation of a particular paper not on the list, we have to ask the member concerned to bear the full commercial costs of the translation, unless it is one which we have already earmarked for translation.

If you would advise us which particular papers you are interested in, we can let you know whether we intend to commission a translation. Otherwise we will give you a quotation for obtaining one.

Yours faithfully

Enc

UNIT 15

Passage 6

MEMORANDUM

From   Secretary   Ref   JJT/PT
To   Dr P R Henderson   Date   21 June 1983

TABLING OF SUBCOMMITTEE REPORTS

I have repeatedly drawn the attention of secretaries of subcommittees to the requirement that reports for discussion at subcommittees must be circulated before the meeting, preferably giving the members two weeks in which to read them before attending the meeting. I appreciate that problems sometimes arise and have given instructions that, if a report cannot be circulated two weeks before the subcommittee meeting, I should be informed as early as possible that there is likely to be a problem. I can then make sure that everyone is alerted and that the best efforts are made by all concerned to retrieve the situation.

I was very surprised, therefore, on attending a recent meeting of the Quality Control Subcommittee, to find that three out of the four reports to be discussed were all tabled. I had not been informed of any difficulty nor that these papers would not be circulated in advance.

I regard the failure to circulate the documents as a serious discourtesy to members of the subcommittee, and I would like to have some comment as to why I was not informed and an assurance that this will not happen again.

UNIT 15

Passage 7

21 June 1983

Mrs H Small
120 Chestnut Avenue
HEREFORD
HR2 6AZ

Dear Madam

Thank you for your letter of 8 June drawing our attention to the discrepancy in colour between the quilt cover and the curtains we sent you.

We have checked our stocks of the curtains and confirm that those labelled pink are indeed brown. We have now taken this up with our suppliers and expect to receive new stocks of pink curtains in the near future.

In the meantime perhaps you would be good enough to return the brown curtains by parcel post, using the FREEPOST address label enclosed, and we will forward replacement pink curtains when we receive these.

We apologise for the inconvenience caused and hope that you will be completely happy with the matching curtains when they arrive.

Yours faithfully
PRAXITELES MAIL ORDER PLC

Customer Relations Department

Enc

UNIT 15

Passage 8

21 June 1983

Mrs J J Green
18 Elm Way
Bishampton
PERSHORE
Worcs
WR10 2LX

Dear Mrs Green

REGISTRATION No 050846 - SCHEME A

Thank you for your letter of 10 June 1983. I regret to say, however, that
the subscription rate which was quoted is correct.

The general increase in the subscription rate is due to the rising level of
claims caused by the increase in medical costs. Your scheme also comes
into a higher subscription band now that your husband is over fifty years
of age.

I regret that there is no possibility of a reduction in your subscription
rate as you already receive the maximum 15% discount. You may wish to
consider transferring to the new Hospital Care Only scheme, which many of
our subscribers are finding an attractive proposition.

To help you in your decision, I am enclosing details of all the schemes
available to you.

Yours sincerely

SUBSCRIPTIONS MANAGER

Encs

Reference Section 1

Capital letters; Open punctuation

You have already been using capital letters at the beginning of each sentence. In addition you use capital letters for:

Names of people (and their titles)	Mr John Barrington Susan Mary Hardy Lord Michael Hammond
Names of places	United States (USA) United Kingdom (UK) France
Months of the year and Days of the week	Friday, 20th March Wednesday, 14 June

In business companies and government offices, rules may vary about the use of capital letters for the job titles of people. As a general rule it is probably best to use capital letters — or more accurately "initial capitals" — for job titles when referring to one specific person:

Job titles	Our Managing Director is Mr Robert Smythe. The Permanent Secretary to the Treasury wrote to the Prime Minister. The Sales Manager's Secretary, Miss Katy Smith, has been promoted.
but not	There are now over two hundred secretaries in our office. There was a conference for sales managers in Brighton last week.

Company or company? As with job titles, we usually use a capital letter when referring to one specific company as in:

Company	It is the policy of our Company to take up references for all new staff.
company	The manager made a note of the name of any company which sold word processors.

(You may find when you start work that there is a "house" style on the use of capital letters for job titles, company and similar words.)

When the use of capital letters (initial capitals) is not clear, the person dictating may actually tell you by saying "initial capital(s)" before the word(s). You should then begin those words with capital letters — not just once when asked to do so, but you must remember to do so throughout the piece of work.

Please note the difference between the following instructions:

(initial capitals)	Mr John Smith
(capital letters)	MR JOHN SMITH

Practise for initial capitals

Type out the following task in double-line spacing on A5 with the correct capitalization (capital letters). Ask your teacher to check this work.

on friday, mr p johnson leaves gatwick airport for his business trip to europe. he will visit france, switzerland, austria and czechoslovakia. next march he will carry out a similar tour of africa, starting in lagos, nigeria. mr johnson is sales manager for apex products limited. when abroad he normally stays in hilton hotels if possible. he hires his cars from avis or hertz car rentals.

Note on open punctuation

The model answers in this book are typed in open punctuation. "Open punctuation" means that you leave out (omit) punctuation from:

1. Recognized abbreviations as in the following examples:
   Mr P Smith   BBC   etc   eg   ie   RSPCA
2. The name, address, date, reference, salutation (Dear Sir) and complimentary close (Yours faithfully) of a letter.

The purpose of open punctuation is to speed up typing by leaving out unnecessary stops and commas. You DO NOT omit punctuation which is part of the grammar of the sentence, ie, stops and commas in the main body of the letter, report etc. If you have not covered this in your Typing theory, you will notice this in practice when you mark the tasks in this book.

When you have finished studying this section, return to the Notes to Task 3:2.

Reference Section 2

Plurals

As you know, in the English language, "s" is added to a word to make it plural:

> girl — girls;   place — places;   plan — plans

There are some exceptions:

1. Words that end in "y" usually take "ies":

company	companies
lady	ladies
duty	duties **but not** chimneys

2. Words that end in "o", usually take "oes":

cargo	cargoes
embargo	embargoes **but not** kilos, radios
potato	potatoes

3. Words that end in "x" and "ch" usually take "es":

box	boxes
hoax	hoaxes
batch	batches
coach	coaches

4. Words that end in "ss", usually take "es":

business	businesses
guess	guesses
stress	stresses

5. Some words are irregular:

man	men
child	children
memorandum	memoranda
crisis	crises (similarly — analysis and basis)

If you know the correct plural, you will find it easier to understand the correct use of the apostrophe (Reference Section 8).

Reference Section 3

Use of the comma

The use of the comma is decreasing, but it is obviously still important for the audio- or shorthand-typist to know when it is essential to use one. It is, however, recognized that it is often difficult for the audio-typist to know where commas should be inserted. This is because, if the sentence is long, she may not listen to the whole of it and therefore cannot anticipate how the sentence will develop. In an examination, therefore, you will only be penalized:

1. For leaving out a really essential comma;
2. For putting in a comma where it is completely unnecessary — where it breaks the flow of the passage.

From the point of view of an examination, therefore, you need only insert commas where they are strictly necessary. If you are not certain whether or not a comma should be inserted, the best policy is to leave it out. If you decide, on checking, that a comma is necessary after all, you can "squeeze" one in at the appropriate point.

In an office you must, to some extent, adapt yourself to the style of your employer. If your boss prefers to use additional commas which, although not essential, he feels aid the reading, he may insert them in ink, or ask you to "squeeze them in". Thus you can learn his style.

Avoid over-zealous use of commas. One RSA Examiner wrote in his report on an audio-typing examination that commas were "scattered about at random" by the candidates. Instead of helping the reading, they were "so many hazards to be negotiated, in an attempt to arrive at the true meaning of the passage"!

Essential commas

1. To separate a number of adjectives (descriptive words):
   (a) She was a careless, tactless, thoughtless secretary.
   (b) The Radio Officer is an accurate, fast typist.
2. To separate lists of items in a sentence (though not usually before "and"):
   (a) Order paper, string, glue and staples from the stationery office.
   (b) The Chairman discussed the Company's assets, liabilities, overseas investments and reserves.
   (c) The outstanding position of the firm is shown by its increased profits, record dividends, mounting reserve fund and first-rate sales figures for the year.

3. To separate words or phrases used as an explanation or description (in apposition). This often occurs when giving people's names or statuses:
   (a) Our Manager, Mr. Jones, will deal with your complaint.
   (b) Mr. Green, a keen golfer, opened the Sports Club Bazaar.
   (c) The Secretary of the Company, Mrs. Thomas, was asked to speak.
   (d) Mr. Bright, a Director of the Company for 20 years, was presented with a gold watch.
4. Where there is a change of subject within the sentence. You should notice these, because the person dictating will make a distinct pause.
   (a) The goods being out of stock, the order was cancelled.
   (b) The Chairman having read the Report, the Shareholders gave a vote of thanks.
   (c) Referring to the Contract, Mr. Johnson said the price was favourable.

Use of the comma with open punctuation

As you know from your typing lessons, commas are omitted from addresses (and everything else not in the "body" of the letter) when using the fully-blocked, open-punctuation style of typing. However, if an address is given in the body of a letter, report or memo, commas are necessary to separate the items (under Rule 2 above). Full stops after abbreviations can be omitted.

   (a) The Annual General meeting of the Company was held at the Grand Hotel, Park Road, Gloucester, GL6 5BN, on 16 March.
   (b) Further to your enquiry, Mr. Brown's full name and address are: Mr K K Brown, BA, 10 Oaklands Court, Ridge Way, London, SW15 5BA, Tel No 788 4412.

If the address were displayed in an open punctuated letter you could leave out the commas:

Further to your enquiry, Mr Brown's full name and address are as follows:
Mr K K Brown BA
10 Oaklands Court
Ridge Way
London SW15 5BA
Tel No 788 4412

The displayed method of giving addresses is preferable.

Note: Commas have been used sparingly in this book to train you to see where most people would agree that a comma is needed. You may, of course, use more commas than those shown, if you are certain that you are using them correctly.

Reference Section 4

Letter display

1. There are many different types of display in use, but the most common ones are those illustrated below on page 79. The fully-blocked, open-punctuated style is the one adopted for the worked answers in this book.

2. You should use whichever style your teacher prefers you to use. If you use the traditional style, you must pay special attention to your punctuation of the address, etc.

3. Take one carbon copy of each letter, unless otherwise instructed.

4. Names, addresses, references and the date are not normally dictated to you. In an examination, these are printed on the question paper. In an office, this information is usually found on the correspondence or file handed to you with the cassette. In this book, addresses, references and other information are given in the Notes to Tasks.

5. If only one reference is given, there is no need to preface it with the words "Our Ref." There is no full stop at the end of a reference, whether or not you use open punctuation.

6. Note that "For the Attention of . . ." is placed **above** the address or **above** "Dear Sirs,". It is always followed by the salutation "Dear Sirs," since it is the Company which is being addressed — the letter being for the attention of the individual, and not **to** him.

7. Headings to letters are dictated after the salutation. They are preceded by the instruction "heading".

8. The name of the firm, if dictated, comes immediately below the complimentary close in blocked capitals. This may be followed by the name or position of the person signing the letter. It is important, if any of these items are dictated, that they are placed correctly. For example:

Yours faithfully   Yours faithfully,
JOHN BROWN & CO. LTD.,

                        Managing Director

                        Yours faithfully,

                        John Brown

You omit the punctuation, if using the open-punctuated style. Leave 4 spaces for signature if using A5; 5 or 6 if using A4.

9. You must remember to type "Enc(s)." at the bottom of the letter if enclosure(s) are mentioned, or indicate enclosures in any other acceptable way. This is not dictated to you. It is important to do this because it leads to loss of marks in an examination. In an office, its omission often results in failure to enclose the appropriate documents with the letter.

Note: For further information on open punctuation, see the notes to Reference Section 1.

Our ref. JKF/MM
Your ref. KB/PP   19 March 198-

Turner & Black Ltd.,
34-36 Brick Lane,
St. Albans,
Herts.   ALl 3ND

For the attention of Mr. K. Black

Dear Sirs,

                    Your Order No. A3216

        We apologize for the delay in replying to
your letter of 10 March. Unfortunately the goods
you requested are not in stock and we do not
expect delivery for several weeks. We return your
cheque herewith.

        We suggest you contact Mr. R. H. Thompson of
I.M.B. Ltd. (Tel. No. 44234), who may be able to
meet your exact requirements.

                              Yours faithfully,
                              DIRECT SUPPLIERS LTD.,

                              J. K. French
                              Sales Manager

Enc.

Our ref JKF/MM
Your ref KB/PP

19 March 198-

FOR THE ATTN OF MR K BLACK

Turner & Black Ltd
34-36 Brick Lane
St Albans
Herts
ALl 3ND

Dear Sirs

YOUR ORDER NO A3216

We apologize for the delay in replying to your
letter of 10 March. Unfortunately the goods you
requested are not in stock and we do not expect
delivery for several weeks. We return your cheque
herewith.

We suggest you contact Mr R H Thompson of IMB Ltd
(Tel No 44234), who may be able to meet your exact
requirements.

Yours faithfully
DIRECT SUPPLIERS LTD

J K French
SALES MANAGER

Enc

Reference Section 5

Dictating conventions

Listed below are the dictating conventions of the Royal Society of Arts. You have already learned some of them. The remainder will be introduced in the next set of tasks you complete.

1. The start of a new paragraph will be indicated by the word "paragraph".
2. The following punctuation marks will be dictated: full stops, question marks, colons, semi-colons, dashes, exclamation marks and hyphens. For example:

   This year's results are in line with the consistent growth of the Company, attributable to two main factors: (colon) our massive investment in development; (semi-colon) and our concern for the goodwill of our customers and staff. (full stop)

   Sales have increased by fifty million pounds — (dash) a first- (hyphen) rate result.

   An incredible figure! (exclamation mark)

   Are you sure? (question mark)

3. Commas will not be dictated.
4. Parenthesis (brackets) will be dictated as "open brackets . . . close brackets" and inverted commas as "open double (or single) quotes . . . close quotes". For example:

   The dividend is twenty per cent (open brackets) (as compared with fifteen per cent last year). (close brackets, full stop)

   I saw your advertisement in (open single quotes) 'The Guardian' (close quotes) yesterday. (full stop)

5. The solidus (stroke) will be dictated as "oblique". For example:

   Dear Sir/ (oblique) Madam

6. The apostrophe will not be dictated. (See Reference Section 8.)
7. The person dictating will use the instruction "initial capitals" when these are required. In cases where capital letters are arbitrary, candidates will not be penalized, provided their use of capitals is consistent. (See Reference Section 1.)

8. The spelling of unusual words will be given after the word has been dictated. For example:

   The manager of the Company is Mr. James Foulkes (F O U L K E S)

   The Post Office phonetic alphabet can be used only when dictating single letters, such as P and B, which need differentiation. For example:

   Mr. P. (for Peter) B. (for Benjamin) Farmer

   Mr. F. (for Frederick) S. (for Samuel) Graeme (G R A E M E)

   The P.O. phonetic alphabet is given here:

A for Alfred	J for Jack	S for Samuel
B for Benjamin	K for King	T for Tommy
C for Charlie	L for London	U for Uncle
D for David	M for Mary	V for Victory
E for Edward	N for Nellie	W for William
F for Frederick	O for Oliver	X for X-ray
G for George	P for Peter	Y for Yellow
H for Harry	Q for Queen	Z for Zebra
I for Isaac	R for Robert	

9. Instructions for headings will precede the words of the heading. For example:

   (centred heading, closed capitals, underscored)
   <u>MONTHLY SALES RETURNS</u>

   (side heading, initial capitals, underscored)
   <u>January Sales Figures</u>

10. Words to be underscored in a sentence will be dictated and then followed by the instruction "underscore". For example:

    This morning's issue of the <u>Daily Telegraph</u> (underscore Daily Telegraph)

11. The typist should adopt normal practice in typing numbers, dates, etc., but where figures or words are specifically required, this will be indicated by an instruction "figure" or "words". For example:

    The population of Gibraltar is (figures) 30,000.
    Dated this (words) twentieth day of June nineteen hundred and seventy-four

    The twenty-four hour clock will be dictated as spoken, but should be typed in the normal way. For example:

    seventeen hundred hours = 1700 hrs.
    oh six twenty hours = 0620 hrs.

12. Pounds sterling will be preceded by the words "pound sign". For example:

    (pound sign) two point seven five = £2.75
    (pound sign) oh point five two £0.52

13. An examiner may require abbreviations to be dictated so as to show whether or not stops are required. For example:

    c. (stop) i. (stop) f. (stop) = c.i.f.
    Order No. BA. (stop) 4231 = Order No. BA.4231
    (capital letters) BBC = BBC
    (capital letters) R. (stop) S. (stop) P. (stop) C. (stop) A. (stop) = R.S.P.C.A.

Reference Section 6

Memo display

M E M O R A N D U M

From	Author	*Ref*	MP/mp
To	Student	*Date*	Today's

MEMO DISPLAY

The memo you are reading is set out in the fully-blocked style. There
are many ways of displaying a memo, but this style is probably the
quickest and easiest.

Many companies use memo forms, some of which have dotted lines and
these must be completed with care.

In some firms memos are signed or initialled: in others they are left
blank. Enclosures should be indicated as usual.

MEMORANDUM

To ..Student...................   Ref ....MP/MA............

From Author..................   Date ...Today's...........

Subject ...Memo Display.................................

This is an example of a memo form with dotted lines. You must be careful,
when completing the items, that the line of typing is just ABOVE the dots.
The typing should not sit on the lines, nor be too far above.

When using a memo form you can adapt your margins to the headings on the
form. The subject item may be centred, but this is not necessary.

Reference Section 7

Indexing

What is indexing?

The purpose of indexing is to let the audio-typist know in advance roughly how long each piece of work will be. It should help her plan her work and should help her decide when to use A5 paper rather than A4.

Methods of indexing

The person dictating can mark the beginning of each passage on the index, thus showing roughly how long each dictated passage lasts. There are several different methods of doing this. The index itself is divided into sections, usually covering the number of minutes dictation on the cassette. So each time the beginning of a passage is marked, it will show how many minutes the preceding passage took on the cassette.

The index may be a slip of paper which is completed by hand by the person dictating. More likely nowadays it will be completed by pressing a button on the microphone to mark off the sections on a magnetic strip fixed on to the cassette itself (see Fig. 1). Or it may mark off sections on a special piece of paper or index strip attached to the dictating machine.

All this sounds very complicated, and is much better explained to you by your teacher who can demonstrate indexing – preferably on several different machines.

Modern electronic indexing will also indicate any special messages, such as those about mistakes made by the person dictating. In fact, the tape may, when put into the machine, automatically wind itself to the place where the dictator has left an "error message" or some other important instruction, so that you can hear this first.

Problems in using indexing

Remember however that index slips only show the number of minutes the dictator took over each passage and not the speed

Fig. 1 Cassette with magnetic strip showing 14 minutes marked off for 3 tasks

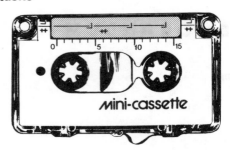

of dictation. A letter dictated at 120 wpm will take up exactly the same amount of space on the cassette (and therefore on the index), as one twice its length but dictated at 60 wpm.

Because of the unreliability of indexing, you may find that it is not used in some companies. Instead, the length of the task may be indicated by the person dictating saying "This is a short memo to . . ." or "This is a long letter to . . .", etc. In other companies, only A4 paper is used to avoid decisions on paper size. Of course this results in some very short letters being poorly displayed. It is probably only suitable to do this when the work is routine and lower standards of display (but not accuracy) are acceptable.

Indexing and this course

Your teacher will decide whether to index the course material and may do so from now on. In the notes to tasks until you reach the examination material, any task which would look best displayed on A5 will be referred to as a "short" memo or letter. You should use A4 for other tasks.

Reference Section 8

The apostrophe

As an audio-typist you must know when a word ends with an "s" whether it needs an apostrophe or not. For example, when you hear the word "companies" it could be:

 (a) companies — an ordinary plural (two companies)
 (b) company's — the singular possessive (a company's offices)
 (c) companies' — the plural possessive (two companies' offices)

Here are some more examples:

 (a) Five companies were listed as manufacturers of televisions.
 (b) The company's staff were told by the Managing Director that they would get a bonus.
 (c) Several companies' figures for the year were compared by the accountants, who found that the top firm was Brown & Jones.

For the audio-typist, the problem is sometimes complicated because she may not know whether a person dictating is talking about, for example, the company's offices or the companies' offices. However, this can almost always be gained from the context. You may have to work out whether a word is singular or plural from what has been previously said, or you may have to listen on ahead a little to find this out.

Rules

1. You do not need an apostrophe if the word ending in "s" is merely a plural. The apostrophe indicates possession (it shows that something belongs to somebody).

2. For a singular word — to make it possessive: **add the apostrophe and "s"**

 The books of the boy = The boy's books
 The pen belonging to the girl = The girl's pen

3. For a plural word (which already has an "s" at the end of it): **add the apostrophe only**
 The books of the boys = The boys' books
 The pens belonging to the girls = The girls' pens

4. To test whether a word is possessive or not you can change the word order of the sentence. If it can include the word "of" (meaning "belonging to"), it is possessive.

 the company's offices = the offices of the company
 the girls' pens = the pens of the girls

5. Be careful with words which have unusual plurals. (See Reference Section 2, if necessary.)

 the man's car = the car belonging to the man
 the men's car = the car belonging to the men
 the child's book = the book of the child
 the children's book = the book of the children

Since these unusual plurals do not end in "s" already, you have to **add an apostrophe and an "s"**

6. Technically, it is accurate to use apostrophes in the following phrases dealing with time, but in practice these apostrophes are sometimes omitted:
 four weeks' holiday = holiday of four weeks
 three months' notice = notice of three months
 five years' experience = experience of five years
 You may be penalized in an examination for not using apostrophes in these cases, so it is best to use them. Note that, in the singular, apostrophes are essential in these phrases:
 one day's grace
 yesterday's date
 one year's trial
 This is because there can only be one day, one yesterday or one year, and it looks strange to have one days, one yesterdays or one years.

To sum up

The apostrophe shows that something belongs to someone or something.
 Singular words (and plurals which do not end in "s") = **add: 's**
 Plural words (which already end in "s") = **add: '**
If in doubt — leave it out: As with the commas, it is not difficult for your boss to insert an apostrophe in ink if you do not put one in. Putting in an apostrophe where it is not needed is a more serious error.

Its and it's

These words confuse many people. In its possessive form, there is no apostrophe.

 The dog ate its dinner.
 The firm held its annual meeting.

"Its" is a possessive pronoun — none of which take the apostrophe.
i.e. mine, yours, his, hers, its, ours, yours (plural), theirs.

"It's" is a shortened version of "it is".

 It's a long way to Tipperary! = It is a long way to Tipperary!
 "Put the machine down where it's useful — on its desk."

Thus, the word "it's" is rarely used in dictation in business offices, and if it is said in the speed of normal dictation, it would almost always be typed back in its formal style, as "it is". If you hear:

 "Dear Sir, It's a long time since we heard from you . . . ."

You would actually type:

> Dear Sir,
> It is a long time since we heard from you . . .

Note: In this book, the word "it's" will not be dictated, so do not use this form.

Exercise

Try the following examples by writing in a possessive form of the word given in brackets:

1. (company) The . . . . office is in the High Street.
2. (director) The . . . . car was parked in the wrong place.
3. (secretary) All the . . . . typewriters were replaced with new models.
4. (women)   The company sells . . . . clothes.
5. (month)   The goods will arrive in one . . . . . . time.

The answers to these examples are given in the Notes to Task 9:1.

Reference Section 9

Similar-sounding words (homophones)

By now you will have noticed that some words which sound the same have different spellings and meanings. You have already met the words check and cheque, and also the word "stationery", referring to paper and envelopes: this is sometimes confused with "stationary", meaning "not moving". There are a number of words like this, and the main ones you will meet in an office are listed below.

adverse	averse	hire	higher
affect	effect	lead	led
canvas	canvass	lose	loose
cereal	serial	licence	license*
council	counsel	practice	practise*
chose	choose	plain	plane
currant	current	past	passed
draft	draught	principal	principle
dependant	dependent	site	sight
ensure	insure	stationary	stationery
elicit	illicit	there	their
formally	formerly	whether	weather
check	cheque		

*licence and practice are nouns
to license and to practise are verbs (doing words)

You will know the meanings of most of these words but if there are any you need to check, use your dictionary. When you are sure you know the differences between each pair, you can try the following exercise. Cross out the **wrong** word of each pair, to leave a correct sentence.

1. Mr. Thompson is the **principal/principle** of the College.

2. Will you **ensure/insure** that a **license/licence** is obtained before exporting the goods?

3. The date has **past/passed** for renewing the **license/licence**.

4. **Adverse/averse** **weather/whether** conditions can - **effect/affect** the crops — especially **serials/cereals**.

5. The Export **Council/Counsel** for Europe said **their/there** regulations did not **defer/differ** from those of America.

6. Please **check/cheque** **weather/whether** the Company owns a building **sight/site** in Ship Street.

Reference Section 10

Examinations

Although only RSA examinations are given in this book, audio-typewriting is examined by the London Chamber of Commerce, Pitman Examining Institute, B/TEC and others. If you are preparing for these examinations, your teacher will give you appropriate practice.

Examining Boards change the style and content of examinations from time to time. The information given below is correct in 1985. Your teacher will tell you if there have been any changes.

RSA I

The past papers given in this book are in two parts:

Part 1 is a manuscript exercise which may require some rearrangement of the material.

Part 2 comprises 560 words dictated at an average speed of 70 wpm. It is usually several passages, eg, one or two letters, a memo and a notice or report, and carbon copies may be required.

Dictionaries may be used.

Before each passage you will be told the number of words it contains and a guide is given at the end of this section, to enable you to choose the correct size paper. (Your college or school may provide you with some form of indexing too.)

If you need to re-type anything, you may of course do so from the first copy you have made. You do not need to audio-type it a second time, as required when you are training.

RSA II

As you would expect, you will have to work faster at this stage. In the current examination there are 800 words to transcribe. In addition, you will be dictated short notes from which you will compose a letter in reply to one printed on the question paper. This is a very important task and it is unlikely you will pass if you do not complete it.

As with Stage I, there is a passage to copy and this may be incorporated into a report, letter or memo — which can make the task more difficult and time-consuming. It is very important that this copying work is also completed.

The speed of dictation averages 80 wpm.

RSA III

In addition to the skills you have acquired for Stage II, you will be expected to complete the work at a very fast rate of production. The dictated speed is approximately 110 wpm and 1,400 words are currently dictated.

There may be grammatical and stylistic errors which need correction. A conversation or meeting may need to be typed out, using correct grammar and punctuation. You may be asked to extract information and/or summarize a passage. This examination requires expert typing knowledge and a high degree of skill with the English language.

Estimating paper size by word count

In examinations, the number of words dictated may be given to you and the following is a **guide** to the selection of paper:

Elite type (12 pitch)
Letter under 110* words = A5
Memo, report, etc., under 150 words = A5
Letter between 110–160 words = A4 with spacious display§
Letter over 160 words = A4

Pica type (10 pitch)
Letter under 90* words = A5
Memo, report, etc., under 120 words = A5
Letter 90–130 words = A4 spacious display§
Letter over 130 words = A4 normal display

---

* This allows for a subject heading or attention line, but if both are dictated you may need A4.
§ Spacious display would, for example, use treble-line spacing between items (date, addressee, etc.) above the body of the letter. Margins could be wider where this does not unbalance the display in relation to the headed paper.

Reference Section 11

Audio with tabular work

Often in an office you will need to incorporate a set of figures, display or handwritten material, into a passage you are typing from an audio cassette. It is not at all difficult to do this: you are told at which point in the dictation to incorporate the handwritten section. This skill is usually tested in the RSA Stage III examination. (Sometimes the completed work from manuscript has only to be attached to the appropriate passage, and does not have to be incorporated. This is, of course, more straightforward and easier.)

Always study the tabulation/manuscript passage carefully before you start on the dictation; it may contain some difficult spellings or unusual words, names, etc., which come up in the dictation and which may not be spelt out for you since you have them in writing — if you care to look! Studying the manuscript passage before starting to type will also help you to understand what is going to come on the cassette.

Unless otherwise instructed, use equal margins for a report or passage which incorporates a tabulation, since this will make it easier to display the tabulation effectively.

Displaying a tabulation in the traditional, centred style is a more difficult skill, as you must allow for any difference in the margins in your calculations. If you do have to use unequal margins, you must also remember to centre headings over the typing and not over the width of the paper.

One of the most difficult aspects of incorporating display into a passage is to make sure that, if you have a continuation sheet, you break the work at a suitable place. It is preferable not to have to divide a tabulation. If no fixed instruction is given, you can use your line spacing to fix a tabulation on to the amount of paper available — using single, one and a half, or double, as appropriate.

If you need help with working out tabulations, ask your teacher to go over this with you. For blocked display the following is suggested:

1. Start the tabulation on the same left-hand margin as the report, letter or memo in which it occurs.
2. Count out the longest line in each column.
3. Allow 3 spaces between each column (can be varied, if necessary).
4. Set a tab stop at each of the longest lines plus 3 spaces.

Reference Section 12

Writing letters from dictated notes

This is a very important skill which a secretary should acquire, since an ability to deal with routine correspondence from dictated notes will save a manager a lot of dictating time.

In the RSA Stage II examination, an exercise on this aspect of secretarial work is given a large proportion of the marks. Therefore, in the examination, you **must** allow yourself time to do this exercise properly. If necessary, do it before completing the dictated passages, so that if you do not have time to finish the whole examination, you will at least complete this important exercise.

You should spend about 20 to 30 minutes on the letter writing exercise in an examination.

1. First read through the printed letter to which you will write the reply. Study it carefully — do not start to compose a reply until you really understand the letter.
2. Transcribe and study the short notes for the reply.
3. Draft your reply in double- or treble-line spacing straight on to the typewriter (do not bother about addresses, etc.) **or** handwrite it, leaving lots of space for corrections **or** draft it in shorthand, if you prefer (but this is more difficult to correct, change and adapt).
4. It is not sufficient merely to string the notes together in correct grammar. Try to improve on the wording of the notes. Fill in any details (although you should not change the meaning of the notes or add anything entirely different). "Pad out" the notes as much as possible — one of the main faults is to be too brief: avoid this.
5. Check carefully whether the notes to the task require plain or headed paper. If plain paper is required, you may be required to type, at the top, the name and address **from** which you are writing. In an office you would, of course, use the firm's headed notepaper.
6. As a general rule, keep to the salutation and complimentary close used in the printed letter to which you are composing the reply. That is, if they use "Dear Sir" and "Yours faithfully", you should also be formal; if they use "Dear Mr. Brown" and "Yours sincerely", you should also be friendly. Remember to use "Dear Madam" or "Dear Mrs. Brown" when addressing a woman.
7. Always start by acknowledging the letter, quoting the date; and end on a suitable closing sentence, even if these points are not indicated in the dictated notes.
8. Correct all typing errors as you go along. The typing and display of the letter is marked in an examination, and is, of course, very important in an office.
9. Do not insert a signature (unless, of course, the letter is from you in your capacity as a Secretary) and remember, if necessary, to indicate enclosures.

Student's production task record

A   Short, simple sentences

B   Longer, simple sentences

C   Short paragraphs

D   Paragraphs (plurals)

E   Paragraphs (commas)

F   A5 Letter

G   A4 Letter (conventions)

H   Memo

I   Letter (apostrophe)

J   Report (confused words)

K   Draft circular letter

    RSA I Paper

L   Memo with Agenda and correction

M   Memo with Table of Figures

N   Letter from Notes

    RSA II Paper

Student's progress record

At the end of each lesson note below the place on the cassette at which you finish:

DATE	CASSETTE NUMBER	POINT ON INDEX	DATE	CASSETTE NUMBER	POINT ON INDEX